Jan ..mas

I'LL BE FINE
ON MY
Own

A SURVIVOR'S STORY

Jan Thomas

I'LL BE FINE ON MY *Own*

A SURVIVOR'S STORY

MEREO
Cirencester

Mereo Books

1A The Wool Market Dyer Street Cirencester Gloucestershire GL7 2PR
An imprint of Memoirs Publishing www.mereobooks.com

I'll be fine on my own: 978-1-86151-268-0

First published in Great Britain in 2014
by Mereo Books, an imprint of Memoirs Publishing

The address for Memoirs Publishing Group Limited can be found at
www.memoirspublishing.com

The Memoirs Publishing Group Ltd Reg. No. 7834348

The Memoirs Publishing Group supports both The Forest Stewardship Council® (FSC®) and
the PEFC® leading international forest-certification organisations. Our books carrying both the
FSC label and the PEFC® and are printed on FSC®-certified paper. FSC® is the only
forest-certification scheme supported by the leading environmental organisations including
Greenpeace. Our paper procurement policy can be found at
www.memoirspublishing.com/environment

Cover design - Ray Lipscombe

Typeset in 12/18pt Plantin
by Wiltshire Associates Publisher Services Ltd. Printed and bound in Great Britain by
Printondemand-Worldwide, Peterborough PE2 6XD

Contents

Foreword

Chapter 1	Beginnings	P. 1
Chapter 2	The gentle touch	P. 15
Chapter 3	Going west	P. 33
Chapter 4	Moving out	P. 42
Chapter 5	Motherhood	P. 65
Chapter 6	Splitting up	P. 83
Chapter 7	Second time around	P. 109
Chapter 8	On my own again	P. 127
Chapter 9	Another try	P. 139

FOREWORD

I started writing this story some years ago when I was living on an island in the far north of Britain. I thought it was time some of the people who knew me were given an understanding of what has happened to me, and why I have made the choices and decisions I have.

In childhood I endured bullying and was sexually abused my father from the moment I began my periods. My life did not get any easier in adulthood, when I became involved with a series of men who treated me badly. In the end I literally had to run away to escape a violent and manipulative husband, and I have children I am not allowed to see.

I hope this book will demonstrate that despite everything, I have achieved something in life, despite a series of men who told me I was useless. I have written it for the children who no longer want to know me, and for future grandchildren who may not be allowed to know me.

My birth name and those of the people who are deceased are original. All others I have changed.

CHAPTER ONE

BEGINNINGS

I was born in April 1963, and I did not have an easy start in life. I was born three weeks early, weighing only four and a half pounds. My mother remembers having to put the bed up on bricks to give the midwife room to work.

We lived in a 1916 brick-built farm cottage, which my parents had been given the opportunity to buy after my father left the farm and went into the building trade. There was panic, as the only phone was in the village, it had been a hard winter and snow was still lying on the ground. My father ran off to the village to phone for an ambulance and stayed to direct them. I had other ideas and beat the ambulance, having already been delivered by a neighbour.

I was whisked off to Windsor Hospital, not guaranteed to survive, and there I stayed for three weeks without my mother, as the doctor advised that she should not be moved. A female cousin had also been born that morning, and my grandfather's comment was 'huh, two more bloody girls!'

My grandfather, Charles Pearson, was a slim man of over six feet, always smartly dressed. I often wondered in later life what he had done in the Second World War – he was the right age – but nothing was ever said, so whether he was deemed medically unfit or in a reserved or secret occupation, I will never know. He and my grandmother got married in London on the night the Blitz stated, so I imagine their wedding night was spent down an air raid shelter. What a start to married life for a young couple!

My only real memory of my grandfather is of him in the front passenger seat of my dad's car on days out, with my brother on his knee, pointing out all the girls in their mini-skirts. 'Cor, look at that one!' he growled. He thought he wasn't a man because he only had three daughters, no son. My brother being the first grandchild and a boy, he doted on him.

Grandpa died of cancer at home in his armchair in March 1969. We were playing outside, being looked after by our grandmother after school. She had locked herself out and my mother had to climb up the ladder and enter through the bedroom window, where she found him.

We were not allowed in, or to go to the funeral. My grandmother, in contrast to her husband, was only five foot one inch, so she must have been at least a foot shorter than him. She had black hair, always with a fag hanging out of her mouth with a long ash, and we would watch it, waiting for it to drop. Sometimes her cooking tasted of ash; I can still taste it now.

I was christened Janice Avril Brown. My middle name was given to me as it's French for April, my birth month, and it was one of the few French words my mother knew. She chose Janice because she liked it, but I grew to hate it. It seemed every time I'd done something wrong the 'iss' was hissed out at me. The name Janice was only given to dim, unattractive women on TV.

I hated it so much that in my forties I officially shortened it to Jan, one reason I avoid visiting family now as they automatically call me Janice no matter how many times I correct them, and my ex-husband did it purpose when we split, knowing I detested it.

One of my earliest memories is of being taken to Spain when I was three. I can remember the gorgeous apricot jam, young frogs in an alleyway where we walked down to the beach and a toy donkey, which I treasured. There was a photo of me being held by my father in the middle of a busy road where the drivers kept coming, taking no notice of him with a small child held tightly in his arms - I believe the Europeans still drive that way.

I started at the village school just after my fourth birthday. It was a small school with only a few classrooms. The infants were taught alongside years one and two. In the afternoon we had to lay down on prickly mats. Twice I fell asleep and remember waking to everyone staring at me, which made me feel very self-conscious. Next time I would desperately try to stay awake.

My mum, in the meantime, wanted to go back to work, and got a job in the kitchen of the next school. She insisted we went there so she could keep an eye on us. This, in my opinion, was a mistake. We did not have any friends in our village; it was a long way for little legs to walk to school, and every time I got into trouble, the teachers went running to my mum. 'Mrs Brown, Mrs Brown, Janice has done so-and-so or been rude to me!' Then I would get a slap from my mother and be told 'wait till your father gets home!' When I would receive a good hiding, two or three times a week.

Both I and my brother Vince, who was two years older than

me, were always getting into trouble for trespassing or vandalism, which resulted in more good hidings, and the police were regular visitors to our door. A mile up the road was the main railway line into Paddington. We played on the railway lines, daring each other to cross in front of a train or put objects on the line, until one day, Vince saw Mick, his English Springer Spaniel, get killed chasing rabbits across the lines. Mick even dragged himself onto another track, where a second train finished him off.

Vince was so inconsolable that my parents went out that night and got him another puppy, this time a Golden Labrador called Penny, but Penny would not settle down, and after a few months Dad took her to the animal shelter, claiming my mum was pregnant and they could not keep the dog. Barry, a neighbour, scraped Mick's body his off the line and he was buried in the garden.

I was terrified of dogs for many years, screaming every time one bounded up to me. Mum would slap me for screaming, even if it was Vince beating me up. That taught me that help did not arrive if you screamed.

The local farm was another play site for us. Once we all got chased from the farm by an old boy on his bike, and I was the first to give up, unable to run any more. He recognised me, and of course reported us to our parents. Another time I threw stones at car tyres and a woman told my mother that I was throwing them at her car windows. The stones bounced and it may have seemed like that. She had a baby with her and naturally was concerned for its safety.

We spent hours playing in the woods, where there were

4

wartime air raid shelters which made great dens, or in the hollows of trees. Making a fire inside them was not advisable, and one burned down. We also went over the airfield, where there were unused buildings with phones still connected, so we phoned people and said silly things. There were some plane wrecks, and we used to play on them until my brother sliced his ear on jagged metal and had to have stitches. The wrecks were moved soon after that.

We enjoyed happy times making dens, sometimes out of straw or hay bales, and often the farmer would jab his pitchfork right through trying to get us out. How he never stabbed us, I'll never know.

The quarry was another play area. I lost my wellies in quicksand and we were lucky we did not drown with all the weed that seemed to reach out to trap us. On one of many fishing trips my brother often dragged me on, in the freezing cold, I fell in when the bank gave way. I could not swim then but had the sense to turn around and grab at the bank. Clumps of grass came away and I yelled to Vince to help me, but he was more interested in a potential bite. In the end two boys of around fifteen pulled me out, one of them getting his foot wet. Vince made me strip off, worried that mum would give him a row for my wet clothes, but being winter they did not dry and we had to confess.

There was berry picking, and Mum would make jam and pies. On a Saturday we often had scones and Victoria sandwich cake for tea. Mum was a good cook but I was not allowed to do any cooking, as my father said he'd had enough of our mother practising on him. I never became a good cook and later I found cooking a chore rather than an enjoyment.

We had to do plenty of chores. As soon as we got in from school we had to change and polish our shoes. Mum would never let us give time for the polish to settle in, so it was hard work to rub it straight off. I had to do the washing-up and drying and put things away, and again Mum made it hard by just piling everything up in the sink while Vince just chilled out. After many tantrums he was made to help me and eventually paid me to do his half. He still owes me around £40!

She started me on the ironing when I was seven or eight, just doing tea towels at first, but by the time I was 12 I knew I had to get on with the pile of ironing before my homework or mum would tell my father I was lazy and there would be hell to pay. I used to weep tears of frustration trying to iron the huge white stiff sheets. Everything had to be ironed, even my father's huge string vests and pants. Now I only iron my work shirts in the summer and still find it a chore.

Primary school was generally happy. I was a popular kid. I usually arrived in a dream and wandered around the playground in a trance. I would turn to see many followers, which would annoy me as I wanted to be alone. I excelled in sports, netball, rounders and the egg and spoon race. Academically I was only average. We had to read to our headmaster once a year and he always told me that I was a year below in my reading. One year I felt really pleased with myself as I knew I had managed to advance in the book, only to be shot down by my headmaster, saying I was still a year behind.

They had stopped the eleven-plus, but we turned up one day to find we were to do a mock one. I enjoyed working out the questions they set, such as 'if a car travels at 30 mph and has so many miles to travel, how long will it take?' He told my mother that I would have made it to grammar school, but I think I would have struggled.

One year we were expected to go to the secondary school to participate in a mass music session, and I refused to go. The headmaster didn't force me but said I couldn't go on the summer school outing either. He knew I really wanted to go but I was too stubborn to back down.

When the summer trip was close I was ill, and my mum had to be called to the school twice before she took me to see the doctor. It turned out I had a kidney infection. We called at the school on the way back to inform them and the headmaster said 'If she is well enough tomorrow, do bring her along as it's the school trip.' I looked up abruptly, shocked, but I was too ill to go anyway. I think that was the only time I saw my headmaster as human. I had not told my mum that I was not allowed to go, and she had left the school kitchens the year before.

Playing netball in the lunch break one day, I made a flying leap for the ball. A girl must have stuck her leg out (she was sitting on the bench right by the goal post – it was Janet, a year younger than me, also very good at netball and possibly jealous of me) which brought me crashing down on my forehead. I could not see properly. I was guided into the classroom and did not know where my place was, which upset the child whose chair I had sat in. Then I started throwing up. Mum was called, and she took me to hospital. My vision had cleared by then and I was more concerned about the motorcyclist in the next bed. I had concussion but was allowed home later.

My parents always thought any illness was faked to get out

of something. One time my Mum had a bug, which I caught, but I was not believed until I was throwing up.

We had close family and took turns to host various events. We always had fireworks. At one village event a spark from a hand-held sparkler went into my pocket and it started smouldering. I remember an uncle bashing hell out of my pocket, but it burnt a hole.

I had to share my birthday parties with my twin cousin or my brother, whose birthday was three weeks later. My Mum usually forced me to clean my push bike on my birthday, and when I had to scrub the rust off the wheels, I always ended up in tears.

My dad was a self-employed builder, who had a partner, Uncle Harry. We were never allowed to call adults by their first names, so it was Uncle or Mr. He was Canadian, married to an Englishwoman. I used to run to him and sit on his knee. I idolised him. He went back to Canada without telling anyone, leaving my father in the lurch.

My parents had many rows over money, and can remember asking what tax was, to be told 'It's none of your business'. We always had to ask for our pocket money, and I used to spend hours trying to get up the courage to ask. If Dad was in a bad mood, he'd say 'You've done nothing this week, isn't that right Mary?' Mum was too frightened of him to disagree. I would not get anything.

He was always telling me that I was a lazy bitch and how much I cost him, and he resented all the weeks we had for school holidays. I'm sure if it had been legal he would have set us to work. He said if he ever won the Pools, the first thing he would do was put us kids in boarding school. I used to pray that he didn't win as I imagined boarding school being like the one in *John Brown's Schooldays*.

Meal times were fraught. We had to stay silent, sit up straight, elbows off the table. My father liked a dry dinner, no gravy or sauce. Mum provided us with gravy but we were not allowed a drink of any sorts, as they believed that kids that filled themselves up with fluid would not eat. This caused a problem for me every time we had mashed potato. It was so dry that it gave me ear cups and dad would whack me across the head, no matter how slowly I tried to eat it.

Mum was a good cook but the mash was often lumpy and the stew was more gristle than meat. However we had to eat everything on our plates or Dad would force our mouths open and shovel it in, choking us. 'You don't waste good food in this house!' he would say.

We had several days out to the beach. To us it seemed to take forever to get there and of course it was constantly 'are we there yet?' On one occasion when I got into my uncle Tony's car, I didn't shut the door properly and asked my younger cousin how to open it. Being three years younger he didn't reply and I forgot to mention it to my uncle. This was the time before any seatbelt law, but fortunately for me cars were also very slow and crawled up hills. Learning against the door it opened, and I fell out. All I had was a large gravel rash on my thigh, but it panicked the adults. For the rest of the trip, I sat in the front with my mum and she made me go into the sea to wash it. Boy did it sting with the salt water.

We had day trips and one holiday to The Isle of Wight. I

really enjoyed that holiday. I made friends and there was a kids' club and we were allowed into the dance hall till 9pm. The hovercraft was great, but I upset my dad by wanting to sit with my new friends. I can't remember their names and never kept in touch.

Other holidays were to Cornwall, and the white chalk sticks in my mind. Once Vince and I were drifting out to sea in a pedal boat, and he wanted me to swim to the cliffs, but I was not a confident swimmer. Eventually someone noticed our distress and a rowing boat was sent out to get us. Another time we were all in a rowing boat and had rowed out near some big ships. Someone dropped an oar and Vince dived in to retrieve it - I was terrified.

Another time we were going to Scotland bed and breakfasting, and after stopping at a service station, Dad accidentally rejoined the motorway going back south again. It was miles before we could turn around, which didn't put him in a good mood.

Mum always tried to get me to wear dresses, but it was freezing in Scotland, with thick fog. We got stuck behind a pickup carrying carcasses, and the driver would not pull over to let anyone pass. The stench was horrendous. At one B & B I spilt my coffee over myself and got a real dressing-down from my mum, I'd embarrassed her again! I was not happy until she let me put a pair of slacks on.

There was also a holiday to Butlins when I was small; I don't remember it but the photo of me sulking was often brought out. My parents sent us for swimming lessons at the local outdoor pool. I would spend all the lessons freezing trying to get into the pool. On one trip to the sea I decided I was going to swim and did it as though I'd always been swimming. Again, back at the open pool I could not swim. It was with winter lessons at an indoor pool near Reading that I eventually learned. I was told I had a good breast stroke.

Mum used to take us to Liverpool to visit a great aunt, where the loo was right down the garden and Vince got a fright seeing her teeth in a glass. I always felt that my dad's mum didn't like me, as she never missed an opportunity to criticise me. Again Vince was the golden boy.

Granddad Brown also died when I was about six. He was a lot older than Nanny Brown, being his second wife. My memories of him were of him being bedridden and staring at us with his glass eye, shot out in World War 1. Sometimes it was left on a dresser, so we always felt he was watching us even when he was not in the room.

He had an invalid carriage, a three-wheeler that you steered with a stick. Once he could not stop it and went right through the garage, and I can still picture the outline of him making a hole through the back wall - obviously it was not brick.

Around this time Mum became ill. If my father had not driven her to the doctor's that Saturday, she would not have made it as she was delirious with the pain. It turned out to be a ectopic pregnancy, and she nearly died. I answered the phone to be told she was in hospital and not to worry, Auntie Bea was coming over to take care of us.

Auntie Bea and her husband arrived with their two sons. My aunt was not the best housewife, and there were buckets of nappies everywhere. I had a tantrum for some reason I cannot recall, and stormed up to my bedroom and slammed the door. It was an old door with a lock, and it locked and I couldn't open it. Many hours later they asked me if I'd like to come down and I said, 'I can't, the door won't open'. My uncle, who was terrified of heights had to climb up to my window and take the lock off. I thought he was going to kill me. I wasn't allowed to forget that, but he was one of my favourite uncles.

A family moved into the next door-but-one house; they seemed a bit rough, he had ice-cream vans. But their daughter Jean and I became great friends, almost inseparable. Once my mum promised to take us swimming, then she broke that promise. I pinched some money from her purse and we cycled to the pool. Jean also took a threepence, although later she always denied it. I could not find my swimming costume, so I swam in my brother's trunks.

On the way back I tried to find a different route and got us lost. A lady came out and let us phone home. Jean's dad came to collect us. He took us to the police station where a huge policewoman gave us a telling off. I was in floods of tears, but Jean was laughing at me crying. Anyway it worked, I never pinched from my mum's purse again.

After Jean and her family moved back to Southampton I went to stay with her as a teen, but we no longer had anything in common and I always felt she was putting me down.

The woman in the middle house was Spanish, and even after years of living in England she could still only speak pigeon English. They had a son, Johnnie, and we really picked on him. He followed us around and we shoved a cow pat in his face. Another time I threw a stone at him, to scare him off, but it hit him on the lip. His mother came round. I was alone in the house and wouldn't answer the door, but she hammered so hard on the glass that it broke, cutting her. The police were called and I was the one told off for throwing stones.

A friend and I spat in Johnnie's face, she then spat in mine and this time my mum had seen her and had a right go at her, saying 'Children will be children, but you don't do the same to a child'.

When my mum was sunbathing in the garden, she would come out to water her bushes and make sure Mum would got sprayed. She never lost an opportunity to report my parents to the council.

Christmas was a time of great excitement. The days to the big day seemed endless. We were kept up late on Christmas Eve hoping we would sleep, but it never worked. We were often awake at 3am to see if Father Christmas had been. Usually we were told we could open one present and then go back to bed.

All the family bought for each other. I was not into dolls but I liked teddy bears and golliwogs. One doll I do remember, which my Auntie Bea bought me, was a doll with a willy. I was so proud of getting a boy doll that I went around showing everyone its willy. Another time they got me an Action Man, but on the first day I accidentally broke its leg, so I was most upset.

There was much food and Christmas and birthdays were the only time we were allowed pop, which is maybe why I have good teeth. I think we spent Christmas Day at home but took turns to visit other family on Boxing day. I don't recall any New Year celebrations in the early years.

It was drummed into us not to get into anyone's car, be polite but turn down any offers of sweets or lifts. Several times as a child I was approached. Mum had an account at a village shop a few miles away, and she often sent us to collect things. Once when my push bike had a puncture, I took Vince's racing bike. There were two full bags of shopping and as the bike was too big for me, I could not balance it, so I pushed it home. As I was passing a derelict house a man came out, asked me the time and invited me inside for a cup of tea. He said he was working on the house. I kept saying my mum was expecting me home, and eventually he let me go. I dread to think what could have happened.

Several times people in cars would follow me, turn around, pass me again and end up asking me if I wanted a lift. I told my parents, but never once thought I should have reported it to the police. Writing this, it sounds as if these were happy times, yet we regularly had good hidings from Dad. He would pull our pants down, put us across his knee and really hit our bare bums. He even threatened to come to the school and do it in assembly. Maybe I have blocked most of it out. I suppose it's good only to remember the good times.

CHAPTER TWO

THE GENTLE TOUCH

I really looked forward to going to the secondary school where my brother had started two years before. Mum and Dad decided to send him to Altwood Secondary Modern, because the school had been made up of the boys from St Luke's, where Dad went, and Boyne Valley Girls' School, where Mum went. I was sent to our area school, Cox Green Comprehensive. Apparently my behaviour had improved in those two years so they thought Vince was a bad influence and it would be better if we went to different schools. This may well be part of the reason, or it could have been that my best friends had moved away or just grown up.

Full of nervous excitement, I started at Cox Green in September 1974, aged 11. The first years had to turn up an hour later, just for the first day. We were put in the hall to be sorted into our classes. There were three J. Browns and it was the third time I stood up that I was put into my class. I'm not sure of our first class teacher's name, but it was either Arthur English or Mr Arthur and he taught English. He was a really nice hippy type, but unfortunately he left after that first year.

I wanted to do really well at school, and make my parents proud of me. The French teacher put an end to that. I joined her class wanting to learn French and with great gusto I repeated the French words. Then she approached the table next to us, saying someone is not pronouncing 'monsieur' correctly. She picked on a ginger-haired boy by the name of Shepherd, and after getting him to repeat it several times, she declared that it was not him. Then she turned to our table and picked on me, really embarrassing me in front of the whole class. I still couldn't pronounce it.

From then on she picked on me and I stopped trying. I hated her classes so much that I tried to fake sickness when we had double French on a Thursday. Thankfully, for the next two years, I had other teachers, but I was put in the dunce class.

She insisted everyone had a French name. I was hoping I could use my middle name, Avril, but we already had an Avril and she was allowed to use her own name. I was given 'Genevieve' and I had to learn to spell it by the next lesson!

She also made me call myself by the French version of Brown, which I protested about. I not only hated French lessons but for decades the French too. Teachers just don't realise how they can influence their pupils. I'm told she just hated first years and was much nicer from then on.

My parents were not interested in anything to do with my school or schooling, just as long as I attended and there were no letters coming home or teachers phoning them up. A form teacher had even told me that he wanted to see them at a parent-teacher evening. He asked me if I'd told them and I said 'Yes, but it went in one ear and out of the other'. They just couldn't be bothered. They had done it all with Vince, and it was too much effort with me.

I excelled in sport but had to drop out of any teams when the clocks went back, as they could not be bothered to collect me and would not allow me to cycle home in the dark.

I liked English, reading books and writing, and if I ever got stuck on a piece of work, I would tell myself to write it as I thought and the words soon flowed. I liked World War Two history and would have discussions with my dad, when he would always contradict what I had been taught. I used to end up in tears trying to get my point over. Now I can see that he enjoyed it – it gave him a kick.

I also took to Biology, and it was for English and Biology that I was put in for 'O' Level. I expressed an interest to go into the sixth form. My father's reply was 'as soon as you turn 16 you can get out to work and bring some money into this house'. I gave up on school after that. I got a D in Biology and a C in English, but I also did CSE English and got a grade 1.

Sex equality came in around 1975, and the Sun newspaper stated that you could demand that your child did subjects normally designed for the opposite sex. Armed with the paper, I went into to see the Headmaster, Mr Lacey, who terrified me. He listened to me and said he'd consider it. On my way out he called me back and said 'Janice, no one demands anything in my school'!

My dad said he'd back me up, but of course he was all talk and no action, so I never got to study metalwork or woodwork. A few girls did, perhaps because they had the backing of their parents.

Mr Lacey kept asking me how doing these subjects would help me in the future. I couldn't really give him an answer, but I now know that having the basic skills would have helped me immensely. Of course five years or so later things changed; I was born too early to benefit from it.

I started my periods on Sunday 12th January 1975, an event that would change my life for the worse. I was first told about periods from a friend, Mandy, who had just been told by her mother, when we were ten. A year later my mother decided to tell me, and when I realised what she was talking about I said 'I already know, Mandy told me a year ago'.

'Why didn't you tell me?' she replied.

'Because I thought she was lying.'

Mandy's explanation had been that you just bleed every month so you know you're not pregnant. To me that seemed a silly idea and couldn't possibly be true. It took a couple of lessons at secondary school before I understood the process of ovulation, and I still think there must be a better way to know if you are pregnant or not. I'm not religious, but if God exists he's certainly a man!

Mum had bought me a pack of towels, so I was just told 'You know what to do'. My periods at times were painful and heavy, and several times I would cycle home to find my bike seat covered in blood. Periods are a curse and can ruin your life. I couldn't go swimming or do other activities. It was very embarrassing as the boys would go around chanting that they wear Dr Martin's and the girls wear Dr White's. Things haven't changed today; the men at work take the piss out of women wearing Tena Lady.

I can remember saying, 'Are you going to tell dad?' 'Of course' she replied, 'He will have to know.' Would it have put off the inevitable? I'll never know.

Two weeks later I as usual was having a cuddle in bed with my parents on a Sunday morning. After a bit mum would get up to make a cooked breakfast, another Sunday treat. That morning my dad started to ask me embarrassing questions: 'Do you know how babies are made?' and 'Would you like to have a baby?'

What was he thinking? I was eleven, never been interested in dolls or prams, a total tomboy! I felt really uncomfortable about this. I mumbled a feeble 'no'. While he was asking me these questions he was rubbing my leg with what I thought was his finger, but I question now whether it was. I can remember him saying 'You won't tell mum about this'. If only I had, maybe it would have been an end to it. Feeling uncomfortable, I soon made an excuse to get out of bed and put it out of my mind.

Then, two days later, he burst into my room, grabbed me, pulled my underwear down and started to touch me. I think I was too shocked to protest much; I just couldn't believe he was doing it. It happened again that week, and this time I was in hysterics and he hit me to shut me up. He would keep asking if I liked it, and I said no but he insisted I did. He wanted me to touch him, but I refused. He would press my hand and mouth to his penis. Most of the times it happened when Mum was downstairs, and I used to pray that she would see us, but I think the risk gave him a greater kick.

From then on I avoided being alone with him. As soon as he arrived home I would rush downstairs to help Mum, and whenever she went out I'd beg her to take me with her. At this time she was only 29 and starting to get her life back, and she didn't want me tagging along. One time I was pleading with her to take me, and she said she would if I put a skirt on, so I rushed upstairs and grabbed one, terrified that she would go without me.

Of course it was not always possible to go with her, so I tried to get out of the house and just wander around all day. I was amazed that she never questioned my change in behaviour.

Another thing I really looked forward to on going to the secondary school was the French trip, which was open to all the first years. My brother had been with his school and he was even lucky enough to go to Italy and Germany because he was best friends with a teacher's son. I don't know whether my parents didn't want me to go or just couldn't afford it, but they waited for me to get up to a bit of mischief – in this case it was having a pillow fight where a pillowcase was torn. 'You are not going to France now!' she said. I couldn't believe it, over something so petty. It always felt like they favoured my brother. If it had been a question of money, I would have been upset, but I would have understood if they had explained.

In the second year we had a new form teacher, Mr Brian Peacock. He was really nice and taught us maths. I knew my times tables and could calculate all right, but I never understood algebra and unless you were going to be a mathematician or scientist, I never saw the point of it.

My father turned nasty, possibly because I didn't give him much opportunity to touch me, and he was constantly telling me I was lazy, useless, fat and as thick as two short planks. I had to ask for my pocket money when Mum was there too or he would want something in return, so I often went without.

All this was making me miserable. Mr Peacock once asked me if I was all right and I said 'No, I feel terrible', so he sent me to see the girls' year tutor' Mrs Nielson. I was really nervous, thinking I was getting a telling off. She wanted me to tell her what was wrong and I gave her a load of rubbish. The only point I did bring up was that my parents would not buy me any more school clothes. 'Look at my shoes, they are falling apart' I said. I had the same jumper all through the school, although I started off with a 32-inch chest and ended up at a 38. To get a new pair of shoes I had to say in a loud voice in the shopping precinct, 'Look at the state of my shoes, Dad'. He angrily shoved a tenner in my hand, but even in the 70s £10 didn't get you much.

Of course I really wanted to tell Mrs Nielson what was going on, but I didn't know if she'd believe me, and even if she did then I could see my mum hating me and I'd end up in a home, which I thought would be worse. Mrs Nielson went on to foster a boy from my class who was in a home, so perhaps I should have told her.

A few weeks later she asked me if I was all right and had I got those shoes. I was really embarrassed, as the new shoes were badly scuffed and she might have thought I didn't deserve new ones.

My father said for years that he was going to build a swimming pool in the garden, but we heard it so often that we thought he was all talk. He started building it in 1975, although it was not ready until the following year, which was a record heatwave. He told the family they had to help out if they wanted to swim in it. My Uncle Ray was a champion brickie in his time, and the pool soon began to take shape.

Then I heard a yell and looked up in time to see the men running. A gust of wind had got behind the end wall and it collapsed, but my uncle took it in his stride.

We could not wait to get into the pool and my father offered a small reward for the one who tried it out first. It was Easter and the temperature of the pool was around forty degrees Fahrenheit – it wasn't heated. Vince dived in first, but I was prevented from doing so by the curse.

It was so hot that summer that we spent the entire time sunbathing and popping into the pool to cool off. Family were always at our house. Someone from the village asked my mum if her kids could use it, but she refused as normally they didn't want to know us.

The Spanish neighbour reported my parents to the council for not having planning permission, but someone came out and told us we didn't need it as the pump was not housed. The man was quite happy with it, but would like it registered as a source of water for the fire brigade. We were told that we were not allowed to swim in it when no one else was home, just in case we got into difficulty, but of course we broke this rule. On one occasion I decided to be brave and dive in. Being a tubby teen I did not liked to be watched, so I checked the neighbours' windows to make sure no one was watching. I made my dive, wearing a bikini, and the bottom piece ended up around my ankles. As I surfaced and reached to pull them back up, I heard a cheer! I looked around in all directions looking for the peeping tom, but I saw no one until I looked up. A glider was overhead, and I knew that from above the water looked crystal clear, so the pilot would have had a bird's eye view. Next time I dived in, I also checked above me!

The big event that year was being allowed to go with the school to Guernsey. All my friends had gone on the French trip, so I knew no one. There were five or six of us to a dorm, and a group of girls chose me as they preferred me to the other girl, who didn't have any friends. It started off well, but my eyesight had weakened in the last few months and it had taken me a lot of courage to tell Mum I needed glasses. I thought that would be another expense – I didn't know children got them free.

My glasses were not ready for the trip, so the other girls thought I was staring at them getting undressed. I probably was but they were all blurred to me. They ended up getting me to whistle in the dark so they knew where I was. I went along with the joke but by the end of the holiday, they were really bullying me and I sought the company of the teachers.

The day we were due home my period had started early and I did not have any towels. I woke a teacher up to get one and she told me to get some from the other girls but they all claimed not to have any, so I spent the trip home worrying that I would soak everything.

I enjoyed the trip over to Sark, where they do not have any cars, just tractors and horses, and we had a trip in the horse and cart. The dining room where we stayed had ants crawling over the tables. I found out that I get seasick. We arrived home late and Dad let me have the next day off school – he didn't touch me when I had my period.

I arrived at school the next day and on walking into the playground I heard 'there she is, the lesbian!' Now even school was no escape. Only two friends stuck by me, Kate and Susan. Susan is now married to a racing driver and their son has gone on to be an F1 engineer.

School I dreaded because of the bullying and home because of the abuse. There was no escape. I could not see a way out, and no one would believe me. There was one time when I took some pills. I didn't want to kill myself, just for it all to stop. I didn't take that many as I knew I might not be found in time and I imagined my father getting rid of my note to protect himself, so nothing would change.

Kate and Susan also had to put up with the bullying, just for being my friends. I felt for them – they shouldn't have had to put up with it. One time a girl was right in Susan's face, goading her, asking why she was friends with me. Susan just stood there taking it. I may not have been able to stick up for myself, but I couldn't stand by and see my friend bullied. I took a swing at this girl and gave her a bloody nose. I didn't think I'd hit her that hard, but she and her friends ran inside shouting that they would tell Mrs Ferris, who was head of the girls.

Susan turned on me and said, 'What did you do that for?' Nothing I said could get rid of the disgust in her eyes, and I felt that I had lost my only friends. I waited to be called into see Mrs Ferris, but surprisingly that call never came. Perhaps they were afraid of having to admit to the bullying in the first place.

I thought I'd got away with it, but two weeks later, again standing in the playground, I felt something hit me from behind. I thought someone had accidentally hit me with their bag, but I turned around to face a mob of at least twenty kids, and there were a few boys amongst them, plus the older sisters of the bullies. They wanted me to fight back, but I knew if I did I would have the whole mob against me, not very good odds and I would have been really stupid to go for it. So they started taunts of 'Coward!' Damn right I was scared.

The teacher on duty noticed the crowd and decided to take the easy way out, sending me to the other side of the playground. I hated him then but I don't blame him now.

Now I had no friends and the teachers were also against me! Kate did tell me later that she and Susan would have dropped their bags to help me out. I did not know that and with Susan's previous reaction, three against twenty still didn't make the odds much better.

My brother got to hear about this and told my parents, who wanted to know what it was about. I just fobbed them off, saying my friend was being picked on.

The fifth and final year at school was not too bad. The bullies' older sisters had left and I think the bullies had realised that they did not have their protection. I was still getting taunts, but from a distance or from the odd immature boy.

I took my GCSEs and the two O levels and left school in May 1979. The week before I announced to my parents that I was leaving school next week and my father's statement was, 'You are not leaving anywhere until you get a job'.

I liked horses and I had lessons when I was primary age; apparently I showed promise. But when one Saturday I didn't want to go, Mum didn't let me go again after that. At thirteen I was helping out at a stables for the odd ride, and a girl asked me to swap ponies. I should never have ridden hers as I was not experienced enough. This pony had an elongated stride and I fell off. It had been really dry and the ground was rock hard. I passed out and an ambulance was called.

I came to with severe pain in my back. At Battle Hospital in Reading they first told me that my spine had separated from my pelvis and I would spend three months on my back. I always thought that could not be right as I could move my right leg, although not my left. After a few days and five doctors, I was told I just had severe bruising and could go home. School had broken up for Easter and I could only think of my stinking PE kit that would be left in my locker.

I had a limp for quite a while and could not stand for long periods with my weight on my left leg. The first night I woke up in the early hours with severe pain in my chest every time I breathed in. It got so bad that I cried out for my mum. In the past disturbing them in the night would result in a good hiding, so whenever we woke from a nightmare we knew not to bother to go for comfort. I tried getting up, but the pain was that bad that I collapsed onto the bed. This brought my brother out of his room and he ran to tell my parents.

They took me back to the hospital, Dad driving recklessly. By the time I was examined the pain had practically gone and I was afraid of the repercussions of a false alarm. An X-ray revealed water in the chest, and I spent two more days in hospital. This time they put me in the adults' ward and my grandmother, Nanny Pearson, was also in there. She had had a fall and broken her leg in three places. She spent three months in hospital, which upset her as she missed her retirement do.

This was another time when I missed the opportunity to ask for help. Once I was feeling better I got stroppy and told the nurses my dad was being horrible to me, but when asked how I only said I had to do jobs. They must have thought I was a lazy attention seeker, I hoped someone would realise something was going on.

I had always hoped to have my own pony, but knew Dad would never get me one. However one day he surprised me and said 'How about a foal?' They were selling New Forest ones for £50, but to my shame I had to agree to let him touch me. He did it while sitting in the armchair, and I kept hoping someone would walk past the French windows. I'd totally let myself down.

I got my foal, and called her April. She was chestnut with a white diamond-shaped star on the forehead. She was walked for miles, and the only things she was frightened of were the combine harvester and traction engine. She was so friendly that when she was old enough she let me on her back without any bucking.

Once before Dad had offered me £20 to let him touch me. Mum was having a party of some sorts, women only, and didn't want me there so I had to go out with Dad in the car. I tried to get him to visit family, but he wouldn't. Instead he drove around for hours telling me what he was going to do with me. At one point I had opened the door ready to throw myself out of the car. That was when he offered me the £20. I was tempted, as £20 seemed a fortune. He'd stopped giving me pocket money altogether after having the pony. I refused and we eventually returned home in one piece.

Once I was 15 I got a weekend job as a chambermaid at the Eurocrest Motel. I even worked at Christmas to avoid being at home. I never had to ask Dad for money again.

In the autumn of 1978 mum started evening classes at High Wycombe to learn to type. Vince was now 17 and hardly at home. He had been in trouble with the law a lot and Dad would beat him, I even remember the police coming to the door asking for the name of whoever was riding his bike. Vince had lost his licence again and lent his bike out. He would not tell the copper, and suddenly Dad came through from the lounge and started thumping him. The copper just turned his back and let him.

We lived in the Thames Valley, and the police were just as bad as the criminals. At the motel a wallet had gone missing, and four of us girls were interviewed. When I gave my name and address, the copper said 'oh Vincent Brown is your brother'. I think he thought I was as bad. He asked me if I'd taken the wallet. 'No, I've never taken anything' I said. 'Well, maybe not this time' was his reply.

I would even get pointed out when cycling. I could imagine one copper saying to the other 'That's Vincent Brown's sister, not got her on anything yet, but we will'.

With Mum away at her evening class and Vince not at home, I was left alone with Dad. He started telling me he was going to hold me down and rip my jeans off me. He really got a kick out of my fear, but I'd had enough. I think it was a matter of time before he raped me and possibly got me pregnant, so it had to stop.

I shoved my feet into my boots and ran out of the house. It was November and freezing, I didn't have any socks on and only my jeans and T-shirt. As I ran up the road I was wondering who I could turn to. I thought of the Moseleys at the farm, but they were good friends of my parents and I didn't think they would help. I tried knocking on the door of an old lady who lived at the lodge to Shottesbrooke Park, but she was not in or would not open the door.

I didn't know who else to turn to, so I just hung around the garages until Mum was due home. About 10.30pm Dad came out, and I ducked down behind a neighbour's car. My heart was beating so hard I thought he'd hear it. He got in his car and went up the road to look for me.

It was now or never. I saw that the lights were on at our next door neighbour's, Mrs Woolford, who was elderly and widowed. I knocked and she came to the door but turned back, so I knocked even harder and she opened the door. 'Sorry to disturb you Mrs Woolford, but you have to help me, my father is trying to rape me!' I said.

'He's what?'

I repeated it. She must have seen the state I was in, as she let me in. I nearly died when she said she would phone him. I begged her not to. 'He's not there, he has just gone off in the car looking for me' I said.

She waited until she heard the car return, and he told her to send me home, but I refused until mum got home. It seemed to take forever and I was shaking with fear, but she presumed it was the cold and turned up the fire.

Her son-in-law with his small child was there. Later I learned he was a special constable, but he did nothing.

Eventually we heard Mum's car. Of course Mrs Woolford had warned my dad of the accusation, so he'd had time to think of something. My mum came around to get me, embarrassed and fuming. She made me apologise to Mrs Woolford and say I had been telling lies.

Once we were out of earshot she laid into me. 'What do you think you are playing at, your father could go to jail!' she said. 'I'm not allowed to have any life of my own, I can't go out for two minutes without something happening.'

We had nearly reached the door when I turned to her and said 'Mum, it's been going on since I started my periods'. She stopped in her tracks and looked at me. It must have got her thinking. Possibly the truth just dawned on her as she thought of my behaviour all these years.

I waited for her to say something, but she just pushed me towards the door. As soon as we got in I made a beeline for the stairs, but she shouted for me to come back. 'We will get this sorted' she said.

I reluctantly went back into the kitchen, where my father was, and repeated that he'd been abusing me. He accused me of lying and said 'as though I'd touch that!' That 'ugly fat teen' again, no wonder I grew up with no belief in myself and no confidence.

Nothing got sorted, it was just his word against mine. I was eventually allowed to go to bed, but my parents stayed up a while rowing.

The next day was a Saturday and I waited for my father to go to work before I came out. Then I heard a knock at the front door – it was Mrs Woolford, she must have been waiting for him to go too. I crept down the stairs to try to listen in to her conversation with Mum. I didn't get to hear much but I did hear, 'I didn't think he was like that but you can never be sure'.

Dad never abused me again and for the first time in nearly four years I could safely go to my bedroom without the fear of him coming in. It bugged me that I wasn't believed and I used to have a tape recorder running, hoping he would come up and confront me and I'd get it on tape, but he never did and the tape recorder made such a whirring noise he would probably have heard it.

The atmosphere worsened. There was constant tension and Dad never missed an opportunity to slag me off. I'm surprised my family never cottoned on that something was going on, as just about every family gathering he would bring the subject around to sex, especially with my Aunty Pat. She and my dad's youngest brother were much younger and my dad fancied her. She was a nurse from Jamaica and her father was Chinese, and she and a sister had come to Britain to work. I can recall Dad asking her what colour knickers she was wearing. She tried not to answer, then he said 'Janice is wearing school navy blue'. I said 'how do you know?' and he replied in front of everyone, 'I was watching you through the crack in the door'.

Surely this should have set off alarm bells – my aunt was a health visitor. He also asked me in front of everyone if he talked while having sex, and of course I replied 'how would I know?' He must have been very confident that I wouldn't tell.

At 17 my brother spent 11 weeks in a detention centre, after a collection of crimes from motoring offences on his or someone else's motorbike to assaults on police officers. He claimed they had beaten up his mates, and living in the Thames Valley it was quite possible.

One incident always made me laugh. He was caught doing a smash and grab, and they were being chased by police. He was on the back of a motorbike, throwing tins of stolen baked beans at the police car. My mum's comment was 'I can't understand the boy, there are plenty tins of beans in the cupboard'!

The detention centre was in Kent, and we visited him a few times. The first was a shock as he'd had shoulder-length hair and they had shaved it off. He said he had been hit in the stomach for not calling the Governor sir.

He soon learned to behave and worked in the garden, where he was so hungry he ate raw cabbage. He was let out early for good behaviour and vowed never to go back.

CHAPTER THREE

GOING WEST

My first job after leaving school was in a packing factory. It was very boring and tedious. There were a few there who were only doing it for cash between school and university, and straight away I wondered if this was going to be my life. Young men in suits would have a go at packing something for ten minutes and then set targets for bonuses, but try doing it for eight hours. We could be packing anything from shampoo to car parts. They shifted us around a bit, timing our breaks and lunch down to the second.

I stuck it for six weeks. I didn't turn up one day and went into Woolworths and got a job there. In many ways it was worse. I had to wear a skirt without any pockets. Our bags and coats were locked away and we were only allowed access to them at lunch and home time. They obviously expected everyone to thieve.

I was put in charge of the DIY counter, which was very frustrating as it was half empty and nothing was getting replaced. I never found out what the problem was. My supervisor was only a year older than me and she decided to pick on me, so it felt as if I was back at school. I stuck it for three weeks, then tried to get myself the sack, as I knew my parents would not be impressed with me jacking in another job.

I started to swear at the supervisor, although swearing was not something I had been brought up to do. I once called Vince a bastard when he soaked me while we were washing up. Dad heard me and he came straight through to the kitchen. I immediately curled up in a ball on the floor and I didn't think he would ever stop hitting me. It must have been a touchy subject, as Vince could have been a bastard had my grandfather not giving them permission to marry – Dad got my mother pregnant at fifteen. Yes, he was a paedophile even then.

I was sent upstairs to the office to explain myself, and through tears I admitted I hated the job, so she let me go there and then. I later heard that my supervisor had been demoted for bullying.

Mum at this time was working in the kitchen of the War Graves Commission head office. I went to see her and told her I'd been sacked for swearing, and this time I received sympathy, maybe because she couldn't make a scene at work.

I soon got another job working on as a forecourt cashier, and I loved this job. We could wear what we liked and of course jeans were my choice. We often worked unsupervised and had a laugh with the customers.

Janet, the other girl, was about 18 months older than me and very friendly. There was another Janice, the cleaner, who did the odd shift at the till. They also sold cars and had a workshop. There was an apprentice who took a liking to me, but it was not mutual. A lecherous sales rep touched me up in his office. Are all men over thirty perverts?

Jerry was our boss, and at first I would get on fine with him, then one day I said in fun something like 'oh, next year you will give me a company car'. He exploded and jumped right down my throat. 'If you don't like it here you can collect your P45!' he shouted. I was shocked, as I didn't know what I'd done wrong.

From then on I tried to avoid him and dreaded him turning up. He would storm in and point at me, shouting 'you, smile!' I used to think, I was smiling until you turned up.

Working there I got to know a lot of people. There was one young Irishman working in the building and he used to go into a nearby café. I said I'd come along and have a coffee with him, and he said 'oh no, women can't go in there with the men'. How backward, I thought, and soon realised that a life with him would have been Victorian.

Then I started to see much older guys. It was a college lecturer of about 52 who took my virginity on a camp bed in the college. There was also Mike, a guy who fancied himself and I think had other girlfriends, but the one I really hit it off with was a lorry driver. Mick was 32, slim with dark hair and owned his own lorry. I loved to travel with him. Unfortunately he was married, obviously not happily, and he had two kids.

Around this time my parents announced that they were going to sell up and move to Wales. They hoped to buy a smallholding and live self-sufficiently. I decided not to go with them and got a bedsit just up the road from the garage.

I lasted three weeks. It was winter and the pipes froze and I was lonely, so I soon begged to be let home. While I was living in the bedsit I was free to see Mick and I would go off in his lorry with him. But back home there were questions and they wanted to know who I was with.

I even tried going out with a younger guy to put them off the scent, but the younger guys just made me cringe. I now realise that I was just trying to find the love I should have had from my father.

Once I went away with Mick for a few nights in his lorry, and my parents reported me missing. When I got home late a few nights later, my father was waiting for me. Before I knew it he had thumped me and sent me crashing into the door handles of the boiler cupboard. I waited for a further assault, but it didn't come. After calling me several names, including 'slag', he stormed back upstairs.

Then Mum came down and said 'Your father is crying, he thinks you hate him'. 'Well I do' was my reply.

He was not finished yet. The following day he made me get in the car to find Mick. I was not sure where he lived, but gave it away when I spied him working on the cab of his lorry. Dad stopped the car, pulled Mick off his lorry and started hitting him. Mick didn't try to defend himself, as my dad was a lot bigger than him. Mick's wife, mother-in-law and kids came out to see what was going on.

If my dad thought that would put an end to it, he was wrong. What a hypocrite! He was probably just jealous that Mick was sleeping with me.

Jerry took us out for Christmas dinner, the first time I had experienced this. The lad who fancied me kept filling my glass with wine, first white, then red. I'd never drunk wine before or had any experience of getting drunk. I was told that I threw up on the seat next to me, but to this day I can't remember it. I do remember being in the ladies and saying 'I don't think I am going to be sick'. They ordered a taxi for me, but the guy turned up in his boss's car and refused to take me. I had to wait for an older car and I can remember going around one of the roundabouts hanging out of the window, spewing. I was most upset that I'd ruined my new skirt.

I was due into work at 6 am the next day. Janet had been called in because they didn't think I'd make it but I was fine, though this was the only time I managed to be fine after drink. With Jerry constantly going on at me I soon announced that I was moving to Wales with my parents, and he was pressuring me to give a date for leaving. House sales never go smoothly, so I was unable to say, but I got so fed up with his badgering that I told him the end of the week. This was in January 1980. I did get a row from Mum for that, and because I'd jacked it in the dole would not pay me anything.

We moved to Wales on the 8th March. Vince had gone with Dad in the lorry to help out, as he was not moving with us. Mum and I were left to lock up and follow in the car, but as we were about to get into the car, the phone started ringing and she went to answer it. It was my uncle to say Bea had had a baby girl, Natasha. Bea was my mum's younger sister. I liked her because she treated us better, as equals, and didn't put us down all the time. To Mum's disapproval she allowed us to drop the 'Aunt' when we were 12. I found it very difficult to call her Bea.

I really liked my uncle too but once, when I was fourteen, my dad had got him to phone me, chatting me up and trying to get me to meet him. I knew my dad was behind it, as I heard him sniggering in the background, another of his sick jokes. I kept asking my Uncle if Bea was there.

My parents' car at this time was an automatic Volvo, and it broke down on the way. This was well before we had mobile phones, so Mum could not get hold of anyone. Being automatic, the car could not be towed and had to go on a trailer all the way to Wales, which cost around £90, a lot of money in those days. My father was not pleased.

The house was up a narrow, steep and winding road, and most cars had to stay in first gear to get up there. The house was three-bedroomed with a cold bathroom that was built between the floors and over a stream. It had its own drive and a small paddock for my pony. She was to be collected a few weeks later. Susan and Kate reluctantly watched over her for those few weeks.

Dad hired a 4x4 and trailer and I went with him to get April. It was a long trip for her and she was very stiff when we got her out on the sea front and I walked her up the road. Mum and Dad took the trailer back, anxious not to incur another day's hire. I think it was hired from Cardiff, or could have been Carmarthen, but when they got there they discovered that they had left the car keys at home, so they had to drop the trailer and return in the 4x4 for the keys. I'm sure Mum bore the brunt of that.

A few days later dad did me an invoice for what I owed him to collect April. I didn't say anything. I just thought, how does he expect me to pay that?

On the first Monday there we went to sign on, and I remember that the staff were not very friendly and looked at us like dirt, although I think they treated everyone the same. Mum soon got a job in the railway station buffet, while Dad was taken on by a builder doing work on the harbour, but he was let go and told his building was not up to standard. The only work he got after that was to supervise some workers on a government scheme moving graves.

I started off on a YTS course at Neyland Technical College, a general engineering course where we got paid. I cycled the thirty miles for the interview, not knowing I could have got a bus. The course went on to 5 pm so we missed the bus home and I had to hitch. There I found out that I wasn't really suited to become an engineer. It was risky hitching. I used to wear my boiler suit so sometimes I was picked up by lorry drivers and often had guys trying it on.

My relationship with Mick came to an end after Dad received a solicitor's letter sent by Mick's wife. He read it at the breakfast table and threw it at me, saying 'you had better watch yourself!' Stupidly I'd written to Mick giving him my new address and she'd found the letter.

I had another relationship with someone who gave me lifts. I can't remember his name but he reminded me of the actor Walter Koenig who played Chekov in the original series of Star Trek, though shorter and beefier.

Neighbours up the road had a daughter about my age. We didn't become great friends but she did introduce me to the Fishguard and Goodwick Explorers' Club, which was run by a couple who took us on hikes and camping trips. I tried sailing but got seasick. Canoeing was better and I went pot-holing, abseiling and rock climbing. I was better at the abseiling than the rock climbing. Many a pot-hole I went down, but I found it difficult because if I wore my glasses they would get covered in mud and I couldn't see, and if I didn't wear them then I couldn't see either!

Barry, our caving instructor, was nice - he got ten out of ten for his butt! We used to pile into a van, where we could hardly move. It was probably illegal. On one camping and pot-holing trip, I opted to sleep in the van with the group leader's dogs. We didn't have tents, it was just sleeping bags under the stars. I never got much sleep as it was freezing and I could not afford a decent sleeping bag.

Thor the dog got very restless in the night, and I should have realised he was trying to tell me something. Too late, he shat all over me and everything else. Nothing worse than dog shit. I got out of the van as quickly as possible and threw up. There were some soldiers camping too, and they just thought I'd had too much to drink. I felt ill for most of the next day. Some thought I was faking it just to get out of the abseil over the viaduct. I would have done it, but I don't think I could have ever bungee jump.

One thing I did do was dive through a few small cave sumps, which was terrifying. I can remember my clothing getting caught for a few seconds. And once you have gone through then you have to go back! One time when I thought I was stuck in a tight spot, Barry said, 'It's all right for you women, your bits squash!' I was instructed to take my helmet and battery pack off. It was an exhausting day for all and I started to lose weight - maybe it was that 'puppy fat' falling off.

There was one member who took a liking to me, Tom, a farmer from Manorbier. It was not mutual, as he looked like Eddie The Eagle – pity, as he was a really nice bloke. I did start seeing Godfrey, a hippy type who was only seven years older than me. He and his wife had just split up. I moved in with him for a few months but it was doomed not to last as he was into drugs, booze and late nights. We soon got fed up with each other, but I didn't want to go home.

I once slept with the group leader and caught genital warts. Godfrey ordered me out of his house after some of the younger members of the club let off a firework inside and burnt the carpet. Naïve as I was, I believed it to be a sparkler. I had to ask Dad to take me back. This time I was informed that I had to live under his rules!

The college course ended and I got another YTS position, working in a hairdresser's washing hair and clearing up. I hated it, the radio was on all day and it reminded us every fifteen minutes how slowly the day was going. The owners were really tight. They were making a mint and I was being paid by the Government. All the customers were given tea or coffee which came out of our tip money but of course they kept the receipts to put it against tax.

I think I was there about seven weeks before I got a job at another garage, on the till, supposedly. One thing I learned about this part of Wales was that they were about twenty years behind the times. Maidenhead was all self-service, Fishguard people wanted to be waited on and refused to meet up with the modern world.

In the six years I worked there, it did improve a lot. I quite enjoyed the job but the owners were on hand constantly. They would only employ part-timers, keeping them under the threshold for having to pay NI contributions. Later on this got to me, along with needing more cash, and I started to help myself to an extra £20 a week. The boss did eventually find out but couldn't prove it. It's something I am ashamed off to this day.

CHAPTER FOUR

MOVING OUT

It was at the garage that I met my future husband and my kids' dad, Owen Thomas. He was working for a local TV and radio shop, delivering TVs and doing repairs, back in the day when TVs had valves and it was often a question of changing one. He volunteered to fill up the van so that he could see me. I don't remember how he asked me out. We never had much money, so it was a night or two out in the pub and the pictures. I remember seeing 'Jaws' with him and crying out in fright in parts of it.

The rest of the time we went back to his place. He had a darkroom built into the garage; he tried to get me interested in photography and developing, but I just wasn't. We would make love on his darkroom floor. His mum nearly caught us a few times, but thankfully, she would not climb the ladder.

His dad was a cameraman, Welsh speaking, and his Mum was Irish and only four foot eleven, very emotional and always on a diet. We clashed – I was taking one of her boys away. He had an older brother who was a PC in the Met and his younger brother was still at school.

Not long after we started going out, Owen explained that he had a daughter. The mother of his child was a few years older than him, and she had told him that she had been in a car accident and could not have children, but nine months later... he said they were going to marry but could not go through with it, but he had a court order to pay maintenance. My mum had heard a different story, that he'd abandoned this girl, so I think she was prejudiced against him. We moved in together some time in 1982.

Back in 1981, things were not going too well for my parents financially and they got into debt. My dad used to joke about holding up a post office, but once when I was looking for something, I came across a pair of replica pistols. I was taken back when I opened the box, for if it had not said 'replica' I would have thought they were the real thing. I often wondered if the talk of holding up the post office was not just talk.

On a Tuesday evening in March that year I was in a Fishguard pub at our weekly meeting of the Goodwick and Fishguard Explorers' Club. This was the only night of the week I went out. I can remember hearing fire engines, but I didn't take a lot of notice, nothing to do with me I thought, even when someone said it must be a big fire.

Next thing I know, I'm told I am wanted on the phone. I could not think who would want to talk to me. It was very noisy, so I had to ask the person to repeat what she was saying. It was something like 'please come home, your house is on fire'.

I think I dropped the phone. Someone gave me a lift. From Fishguard you can see right across the valley to Goodwick and we were shocked by the sight of flames coming through the roof. The road was totally blocked by fire engines and other emergency vehicles.

I went to the first person I saw in uniform, but to this day couldn't tell you if he was a policeman or an ambulanceman. 'My parents?' I desperately asked. 'They're all right' he said. 'Well, we think they are. Your mother was at work.' Of course she was – in my panic I'd forgotten.

'And we think your father is walking the dog' he went on. He escorted me up the hill, supporting me, but halfway up I felt embarrassed by this and broke away from his grasp. I walked down the drive, spied my mum, crying and near hysterical, and approached her. 'Mum?' I said. She turned, registered it was me, said 'Oh Janice!' and lifted me off my feet, crushing me to her. She cried some more, saying 'We don't know where your father is, we jumped when the windows burst with the heat.'

Not long after that my dad wanders up and Mum clings to him, crying, 'the house, a life time of work!' and my dad calmly replies 'Never mind love, we'll build another one'. Even then I thought that was a strange thing to say.

We seemed to be there for ages watching the fire. Afterwards my parents were put up by neighbours at the bottom of the hill, Mr and Mrs Jones. their daughter Ann was just a few weeks older than me and I have got back in touch with her via Facebook. I opted to stay with friends. I lost everything in that fire except what I was dressed in, a pair of jeans with holes in the knee and a baggy jumper of my brothers. Mum had her bag with her, so she had her purse with cards and driving licence. Dad, on principle, never carried any ID with him, so it seemed a bit fishy when a few weeks later he announced that he'd found his driving licence and wallet in the lining of his coat.

The council put us up in a B & B for a few weeks, then we were able to arrange to rent the tiny cottage at the end of our drive. The B & B owner was a bit creepy. I can remember the lights being turned off and back on when I was having a shower and wondering if he had been spying on me.

While we were there we had the UK census. I know my parents had had problems claiming on the insurance, something to do with the house being up for sale and the insurance firm refusing to pay what it was insured for. But Dad now started to build his dream house, or at least what he could get permission to build.

At work one day I received a frantic call from my mother wanting to know if I knew where my father was. I said I had no idea and I suggested maybe he was having an affair. It turned out that he had been arrested. He had been caught coming out of a builder's yard with a load of stuff he had not paid for and the police removed a pile of items from the house. At court he was given the choice of a £1,000 fine or three months inside, and unfortunately he paid the fine!

Before the house was finished, I was living with Owen. Once, while I was staying in this rented cottage with my parents, they went away for a few days to see family. Of course I had Owen to stay but typical of my dad, they came back a night early. I said 'I hope you don't mind but Owen is here'. He was told in no uncertain terms to go, and I even leapt out of the window to chase after him. Lucky I didn't get locked out. I knew Dad had come back a day early on purpose.

The third thing that convinced me that Dad had had something to do with the fire was talking to a neighbour, Dicky

Bird, near the bottom of the hill. He said that on the night of the fire, he had seen a car come racing down the hill, as fast as possible without any lights on. I think my father paid for a few of the men he was working with to torch the place. I always thought I'd get the truth out of him on his death bed but he robbed me of that too.

My 18th birthday was pretty tame. My parents gave me a gold watch, which I still have today. I spent the evening in a minibus going on one of the camping trips. A few months after my 18th I enquired as to what had happened with the insurance policy I knew my mother had taken out for me as a child, paying in fifty pence a month. I was told 'Oh, your father had that'. It was only about £90, but again Vince had received his money.

I had a court appearance shortly after my 18th. Some months before I had been looking after the group leader's dogs while they went on a weekend caving trip – I could not afford to go. The bitch was a Great Dane and Thor, the dog, a Labrador, and they had had puppies, ugly ones. I was just asked to feed them and take them for a walk if I had time. Both dogs jumped the fence and disappeared after having their food. I was not unduly worried, as the bitch would not stray far from the pups and I knew that they often wandered around the estate.

When I returned later Thor was in a terrible state. It turned out he had crossed a field full of sheep and the farmer had filled him full of buckshot, though the injuries were only superficial. I was summoned to court for 'being in charge of a dog that worried sheep'. The farmer had often warned them that he would shoot him and it was unfortunate that I was in charge when it happened.

In court the copper stated that I had said 'I usually let the dogs out' when in fact I had said 'they' not 'I'. As I don't usually care for them I'd hardly have said 'I'. I was fined £10 to pay £2 a week. I was so upset at the injustice of this that I was not going to pay, but my mum let me off paying my keep that week so I sent the £10 off straight away to forget about it. The local paper's headline was 'neighbour doing a favour led to being left to carry the can, court told'.

In January of 1981 I started driving lessons. My driving test was the only test I ever wanted to pass. As a teenager, on the rare occasions when my mum drove me anywhere, I would listen to the sound of the engine and knew when she was going to change gear. I approached a local driving instructor to teach me; he had a petrol account at the garage I worked. Lessons then were £5.50, but he knew I didn't earn much so let me off the 50p. I believe now in 2014 lessons are around £37.

As soon as I started, he advised me to apply for my test as examiners were on a go-slow and with the backlog it took six months to get a test. I had one lesson a week, and on about the third lesson, he arrived at my parents' house and stopped at the end of the drive. Dad was in the process of giving me a row, but I was anxious to go for my lesson. When he finally let me go, I walked the length of the drive head down and automatically approached the passenger side to find Dave Lloyd sitting there. He said he thought I was going to sit on his lap!

My first lesson began by going around a car park and then out on the road, where he did the gear changes. Once I got the hang of going around Fishguard and Goodwick, he said I needed to have lessons in Haverfordwest, where they did the tests.

Sometimes he was able to give me a lift, but most times I had to hitch as the buses never went when you wanted them to.

After a while Mr Lloyd asked me to invite my dad to come along. I think he was hoping that my dad would see that I was safe and would allow me to practise in his car. Unfortunately, with Dad staring at me in the mirror, I drove terribly and even mounted the kerb. 'She doesn't usually drive like that' Dave told my father. Of course I was not allowed to drive his car.

Mr Lloyd seemed to pick on a certain point every week, so I never felt as if I was getting anywhere. A few times I felt like walking out and telling him where to go. The date of my test was the 10th July 1981. Mum actually took me to Haverfordwest for it, and I used Mr Lloyd's car.

I managed to upset the examiner twice. Mr Lloyd had told us where he was likely to ask us to do a three-point turn, but he told me not to do it there as it was too near a junction and by a bus stop, so I moved along a bit. The examiner got annoyed and told me to reverse back, which I did, but I wish I'd had the guts to say, 'I don't think it's safe there'. Later I had to move out from behind a parked car. I was a bit nervous of this so I reversed back a bit, and that also was against his directions. I had to move forward again to complete the manoeuvre.

I really thought I'd blown it when coming down on the St David's road into the ring road, I scrubbed the tyre on the kerb twice because a juggernaut was coming up around the bend on this narrow road.

On getting back to the test station he asked a few Highway Code questions and then told me I'd passed! I was convinced that I'd heard wrong and too frightened to ask him to repeat it, so it was an agonising few minutes before he handed me the pass paper. My mum then said I could drive home, but Mr Lloyd said I'd done enough for one day.

I was allowed to drive my parents' car after that to run errands for them, but I don't think I was ever insured to do so. My parents seemed to think comprehensive insurance meant everything and everyone - it may have done when they took their tests.

They had got rid of their Volvo and had a Vauxhall Chevette, which was written off when a branch from a tree fell on it - think I still have a photo of that. They then got a Morris Marina. I never felt safe as a passenger. There was no dashboard to speak of and I started putting my seat belt on about six months before it became law. This Marina also had an electrical fault and when we went over a bump the lights would go out. You had to bang underneath the dash to get them to come on.

Coming home one night, a lorry driver flagged us down and said his lights had failed, and could he follow us closely the last few miles to the harbour. Mum agreed, but I don't think he was listening when she told him that hers might fail too. Sure enough when we went over the humpback bridge, the lights went out, and there we were all plunged into darkness with a juggernaut on our backside. Thankfully it came on again after a few bangs. It scared us all, including the lorry driver.

My grandmother, Florence Brown, died when I was 18. She had remarried in later life and I was told that her new husband had treated her badly. She'd twice had a mental breakdown. The first time they gave her electric shock treatment, which sounds barbaric but it worked. By the second time this had been outlawed and she slowly went downhill. I always remember her as a large woman, 15 or 16 stone. She stopped eating, and when I visited her in her London hospital, she was down to seven and a half stone and I had to look hard at her face to realise that she was my grandmother.

She constantly hummed the same tune and on leaving I found myself humming it too. I had to recite nursery rhymes to get it out of my head.

Owen and I rented a house at Abercastle, about eight miles from Fishguard. We cycled to work, and I sweated buckets. The house was down a drive and the last tenant had left it in a mess – I even had to clean out the fat from the grill. We did not have a washing machine and I had to do it by hand, boiling the white socks in a saucepan. I thought I was going to crack up, as it was far worse than being with my parents. Owen did nothing apart from cooking the odd curry and I might as well have done it myself as he never cleared up after himself. I felt that I'd gone from my parents' slave to his. He complained to his mother that I wasn't ironing his shirts right and he expected all his T-shirts ironed too and put on hangers. We would fall out and have two-week silences and I'm sure he only made up with me when he ran out of shirts!

Then his mother gave us £100 towards a washing machine. We could not have it plumbed in so I had to be on hand to hold the hose on the tap and then hold the outlet hose in the sink. A few times we invited his family around, but I was not a natural host and found it very stressful. The only thing I had not cleaned was the dust off the toilet roll holder, which was broken so we didn't use it - someone had run their finger through it. Owen said it wouldn't have been his mum, maybe not but then it had to be his older brother's girlfriend Gail, as she was certainly the type. I had hoped to have her as a friend or the sister that I had craved, but she spent all her time making me out to be the nasty one. She crept around Owen's mum Ellie and wouldn't even laugh at a joke unless Ellie laughed. She of course became Ellie's favourite and Ellie made sure she told everyone this within my hearing.

Gail told me that she and Sam were engaged but begged me not to say anything, and then Sam got down on one knee in front of them in their garden making out he'd only asked her then. I had never let on to Ellie, they would have only thought I was trying to spoil things, but I believe Gail did that herself later on and she and Sam with their two daughters moved away.

Even before our six-month lease was up, I knew being with Owen was a mistake but I didn't have the guts to tell him so. When we left the house in Abercastle the owner was there to oversee us leave, and her nephew had let us into the house. She did nothing but complain. It was not clean enough for her, but it was not dirt but mould, and I didn't think that was our responsibility. She went on and on so much that I ended up telling her it was a lot cleaner than when we moved in. She did give me an apology but still kept our deposit, saying we had caused damage. That experience left me bitter.

Our next lease was back in Goodwick, in Cross Street, which was about halfway between our parents' homes. They were end-of-terrace houses with a dead end, and the only thing good about it was that it had plumbing for the washing machine!

We had only been there three weeks and were spending an

evening with my parents (for a change) it was a rough night, with heavy rain, but I wasn't taking a lot of notice. Owen was getting agitated, and I thought he was just making an excuse to leave. He left, promising to come back, and after a while I wondered what he was playing at. It turned out that floodwater had run down into the village and the garage next door had placed sandbags to direct the water away from his garage but forced it to go down our street. At the end there was nowhere for it to go as it was a closed off concrete yard, so it poured right through our house and was rising in the concrete yard out the back. My main concern was the washing machine, but fortunately it worked after drying out.

I'm not sure which parents' house we stayed at, but we soon got another rental at Dinas, which was about six miles from Fishguard towards Cardigan. It was half a house, owned by a very nice spinster lady – I think she enjoyed the company.

At this time we got our first car, which I think was a Morris, bought from an uncle or possibly a great uncle. Owen always put me down over my driving, and I did frighten myself when I was trying to get out of a Y junction. I was so intent on looking the way I couldn't see that I forgot to check the other way. Thankfully the other driver reacted in time, but it put me off for a while.

I used to ride in with Owen to work, but I finished earlier and had to walk. Sometimes people would give me a lift. One was a farmer who lived near us, James Jones, not to be confused with the estate agent who was there at the time. He also had a fuel account at the garage and would bring in his cattle lorry. He was ten years older than me and looking for a wife, and I took a fancy to him. Nothing came of it apart from me embarrassing myself when I started to send him postcards and then phoned him up to have him tell me he was married now. Next time he came into the garage I apologised to him, and he said 'no need'. I don't think I would have fitted in, as they were Welsh speakers and would have wanted his children to speak Welsh. I heard they had two girls, but I think they split.

We then started to look into buying our own house. Tony, Owen's dad, lent us the ten percent deposit and we bought a house in Goodwick for £14,500. It seemed a fortune at the time and we struggled to pay the mortgage. I was just twenty and a home owner. The house was terraced, two-bedroomed in a cul de sac with the primary school at the end of the road. The house needed renovation, and three years later we got a grant to do it up.

The house was nearly up the top of a steep hill, and we were told there used to be a pub at the top of the hill called Stop n' Call. After walking up it, you certainly felt like a pint or two.

I can remember watching telly at home with Owen and his boss one day in 1986 when there was a news bulletin announcing that the Space Shuttle had blown up - it was a huge story because of the woman teacher who was on board, Christa McAuliffe.

We stayed at my parents for a few weeks before getting the keys to our house. My brother was also staying there with his girlfriend, and they married that year. While we were there Vince was arrested by Maidenhead Police, claiming he had broken into Maidenhead Bus Station. He said they threatened to pick on his girlfriend, Linda, so he confessed to it. They bailed him and he had to make his own way back to Wales. He couldn't have done it as he was in Wales, so he got a solicitor and changed his plea. He had evidence of signing on that day, and it was supposed to have happened in the night.

Mum and I were called to court in Reading to testify that he had been at home in Wales. I travelled down on the train, while Mum had gone a bit earlier in the car. In the end I was not called into court, so I was a bit annoyed having had to go all that way for nothing. It was thrown out, as the guy was supposed to have worn an ear ring, and Vince had a doctor confirm that he had never had his ears pierced.

Some years later Vince had a row with gypsies who poured petrol over him and set him alight. This happened in High Wycombe. Instead of getting help straight away, he drove home to his second wife in Slough. He spent three months in a burns unit, and never informed our parents. After getting out of hospital he visited mum and her comment was, 'Have you been abroad, you looked tanned?'

Vince never co-operated with the police either. It was mostly his legs that were effected.

From the age of 19 I started to feel broody. I can remember going to the doctor and asking if I could be tested to see if I was fertile, as there was rumours that Lady Di had been tested before getting engaged and I thought if I knew I was able then it would be easier to wait. I think my doctor tried not to laugh.

When I was 21 I could not wait any longer and 'accidentally' got pregnant. Ellie was in on it, as she craved a grandchild. Owen took it quite well and we went around his parents to tell them the news – they were delighted. At that time you had to have pregnancy tests done at the chemist, and when he told me it was positive, he advised me to go to see my doctor. 'He's very good at dealing with these' he said.

I was ecstatic and again couldn't tell the chemist that he'd got it wrong. On the Monday I went to see the doctor to tell him I was pregnant, but that morning I'd had some dark staining in my knickers; I didn't realise this was the start of a miscarriage. It must have been that night that I ended up in hospital, where they put me on a drip, and kept filling my bladder to bursting point and scanning me. One minute they were telling me all was fine and the next they were saying I had miscarried and they had to do a D & C. It was one of the worst experiences of my life. They even insisted calling me Mrs Brown so as not to embarrass the staff that I was unmarried - how bloody Victorian! I still insisted on saying 'It's Miss'.

I was disgusted to learn that on my records it would be put as an abortion to protect those who had abortions. I could only think that the chemist would think I'd had arranged to get rid of it. I felt like I was being punished for getting pregnant without Owen's consent, and the experience put me off the idea for three years.

Around the same time Owen had an aunt who committed suicide. She was married with two children. She was always made up, the sort that would not even put the washing out without putting her face on. She expected to be waited on and put in complaints to my boss and Owen's mum that I wouldn't wait on her at the garage. In fact when I found out she was his aunt I used to go out of my way, putting on a false smile as I served her. She got depressed and was on some tablets that gave her hallucinations – the tablets were later banned. She walked into the sea. Some said she was a good swimmer but others said she'd had a fright and never went swimming. It was a shock, though I believe her husband was seeing someone whom he later married.

It was a huge funeral, and her daughter collapsed. I thought how selfish of the woman. I was surprised to see myself named as one of the chief mourners, as I couldn't stand the woman. That was the first funeral I had been to.

We got a council improvement grant to do the house up, but the grant was just a fraction of what we spent on it. We extended the kitchen and knocked the two downstairs rooms into one. Owen did a lot of the work with me grafting. When we were gutting the house, Tony came for a visit. He had a new car – he replaced it every two or three years, always a Volvo. He was filming me coming out with wheelbarrows full of rubble. I pretended to lose control of the barrow and headed for his new car, but I really did lose control. I panicked and tipped the load, over just missing his car. Typical cameraman, he just carried on filming. Luckily the new car was not even scratched and Tony was going to send the clip to 'You've Been Framed' but fortunately for me, a fault developed on his camera and it had to be sent away for repairs. The film was never returned – whether it was damaged or whether someone has it in his collection, I never found out.

Owen and I put a box under the sealed-off stairs when we were renovating, the usual time capsule treasure box – that would have been around 1986/7. We got married in 1985, the year after my miscarriage – pressure from Ellie really. 'You two should get married now to give any future children a name' she said. To please them we agreed on a date in July. Tony and Ellie's was on the 9th, Sam and Gail's on the 12th and ours was on the 6th.

We had been to Sam and Gail's wedding the year before in London. It was extremely hot, and Owen (he was best man) and I had to share a single bed. I fell on a pavement and had grazed knees. I got really upset at the reception because I was not allowed on the top table, and felt I was not being treated as part of the family. If I could, I'd apologise for it now, as it ruined their day.

The weather had been wet in the summer of 1985 but the sun shone on 6th July. I had an anxious wait with my father alone in the house, as I was convinced he would use this as one last chance to abuse me. I must be one of the few brides who turned up early at the church!

Ellie tried to take over, and went on about the men being in morning suits. I didn't know what a morning suit was. My dad had a suit made for the occasion but of course, it didn't match. She wanted things to be done as etiquette but would not sit on the head table with my dad.

Shortly before the wedding, I had visited my parents, who were now living in a maisonette in Bracknell. I'd travelled by bus from Haverfordwest to London via Carmarthen and then on to Bracknell. My parents let me borrow their car to visit family and to sort out bridesmaids' dresses. The car was vibrating a lot through the steering wheel, and I had no idea what the problem was. On returning to Bracknell I mentioned it to my father, and he went to take a look. After examining the car, he told me that if I'd driven another five miles, the wheel would have come off!

He appeared to be putting the blame on me, but he had changed the wheel because of a puncture and I found it difficult to believe that someone would forget to tighten the wheel nuts. Anyone else would have driven the car a few miles and checked them again. With my suspicions of the house fire, it crossed my mind that it was deliberate – maybe he was hoping to claim on that insurance too!

Because of how I had felt at Sam and Gail's wedding, I put Gail on the head table. We were going to pay for it ourselves. My parents insisted on paying for the reception, in fact my dad announced that he would not come if he could not pay. Tony and Ellie paid for a bottle of wine for each table and we paid for the rest. We thought that having booked and paid for the church, that included everything else. It was a scramble to get an organist and we had not booked the registrar, nor arranged cars for the bridesmaids to get to the reception!

The vicar had visited us at home, and he asked if I wanted my parents' address put for me, again Victorian attitudes. I was adamant that it would be our home address. The day he visited, the cat walked in with a mouse in its mouth, and he said something about all God's creatures.

When we actually got married he was taken ill and in his place we had the retired Dean of St David's. The reception went well, apart from Tony stealing the limelight and announcing it was their 30th wedding anniversary. My parents felt as if they had paid for their party.

In the evening a Welsh choir who were staying at the hotel joined us and started to sing – I was told it turned into them singing dirty songs in Welsh. Ellie was on videotape saying to me at the church, 'If you don't look after him I will have your guts for garters'!

About two weeks before the wedding Smokey, my childhood cat died. It was a hot day and I think she waited for me to come home before dying in my arms. I cried my eyes out over her. I should have known it was a bad omen.

I have two other uncomfortable memories of being in my father's company. Walking down the street once he put his arm around my waist and slipped his fingers inside my skirt waistband, and I pulled away, saying 'Don't!' He said he wouldn't touch me like that again, but how could I possibly relax or enjoy being held by my father? The other time I reluctantly went with him to Carmarthen, shopping. He bought Mum a bracelet, and in the shop the saleswoman said 'Would the young lady like to try it on?' 'It's not for my daughter' he stuttered. The woman must have thought he was my 'sugar daddy'. We certainly did not act as a normal father and daughter, and I wondered if he realised this too.

I upset him once. I can't remember what he said to me, but I replied with 'And you look like my grandfather'. My mum said I'd really upset him. What did he expect, me to be all 'Daddy, daddy'?

Owen lost his job at the TV and radio repair shop after his boss' marriage broke down, because he ran the shop down so that his wife would not get half of it, so for a time it was just my wages and Owen received some dole as well. He had got in arrears on his maintenance for his child, and a few times she had asked for more money. It used to infuriate me, as my wages were taken into consideration. Since when did it take three to make a baby? This time she not only took him back to court for more money but wanted the arrears. One of our neighbours was a magistrate but he told Owen he could not preside over his case. It was a surprise that he did so anyway. Because Owen was not working he reduced the £9 a week to £1 plus £1 a week for the arrears, and we couldn't have been more delighted.

Shortly after this, she married and her husband adopted the child. As far as I know Owen has never had contact. It was shortly after this that I persuaded Owen to start a family. I left the garage, giving my reason as wanting to reduce my risk of miscarriage. I was surprised that the benefit office accepted this.

When it came down to conceiving a child, Owen changed his mind, so I looked for another job and had an interview for post-delivery person. I didn't get the job but got taken on to cover for someone on the sick, and it soon became a full-time position. I loved the job for the first two years, and in the first six weeks I lost 20lbs without trying, it was that energetic, no time to stop for lunch. I really struggled with The Welsh place names. Folks would have to stop me and say have you got mail for so and so, but the way they pronounced names and the way I read them were completely different.

It was here that I really learned to drive. I'd been frightened to drive in the rain with windows steaming up, and now I had to drive in all weathers and learn to use my side mirrors. I had a few scrapes. I reversed into a gate and hit a guy in a brand new car when I was convinced that he would give way to me. I very nearly had someone skid into me down the Gwaun Valley. When one of the drivers locked the keys in his van, I was able to squeeze my skinny arm into the window gap to unlock the door.

That first Christmas Eve, I went to the pub with them and they plied me with drinks until I was very drunk. Peter, one of the other postmen, decided to walk me home and tried it on. I got covered in mud trying to fight him off – someone passed us but didn't interfere. I told Owen when I got home and he went looking for him, but didn't find him. I was sick and went to bed – at least I didn't have to suffer the in-laws that night.

I hated Christmases, because I was just ousted into the lounge while they spent most of the time in the kitchen. If I ever went through I was always given a drink and told to sit down. Ellie wanted her boys around her at Christmas and Easter. I once said to Owen, 'Next year we will go to my parents for Christmas' and he replied 'it won't seem like Christmas then'. 'How do you think I've felt all these years?' I replied.

My parents had moved back east and Dad got his old job back. They bought a place in Swindon after selling Phoenix House in Goodwick. My parents were fed up with being on their own at Christmas, so they started going on holiday. I think they had some great Christmases and New Years. They had always wanted to do that.

For the third year I was delivering mail, and being last in I got the job of covering for the ones on holiday. Some weeks were good but others not. I never got the hang of the Dinas and Newport run. It took me at least two hours longer and I didn't get paid for it. The regular guy, Richard, would fail to deliver half the mail and leave it in his locker for me. It wouldn't surprise me if he ended up in the office. One guy got the sack for pinching things, an ex-copper too. They caught him with toilet rolls, but there must have been other stuff.

I got bitten several times by dogs, one of which belonged to a lady who worked on the reception at the police station. Farmers would just find it funny if their dog bit the back of your heel. One had a letter sent to him to control his dogs as a van had had six new tyres in a week. I ran over one dog, and I was really upset. The farmer threatened to sue. It turned out his wife had seen it and didn't blame me, but it was several weeks before I was on that round again and I was terrified. The farmer approached me and said 'I think you're frightened of me, here's the dog, just a broken leg and he's learnt to respect vehicles'.

Owen was now working for his dad as sound recordist and on quite a good wage. He decided that we should start a family. At the time I didn't want to, but thought, 'I'm 26 and if I don't agree he may never agree again'. So I came off the pill. I think I got pregnant straight away. I was very lucky with morning sickness, and just now and again felt a bit queasy. I gave up work. The baby was due on the 12th February 1990, but on that date I had a dental appointment. My dentist at the time was my gynaecologist's daughter, so you would have thought she would have known that it is extremely uncomfortable for a heavily pregnant woman to lie right back. I could hardly breathe and didn't know if I was in labour or having a panic attack. She eventually noticed my discomfort and stopped the examination.

Owen didn't go to work that day. I didn't want the baby born on the 13th as it was Owen's birthday, or the 14th, being Valentine's day. At 7.30 on the morning of the 15th I desperately needed the loo, but Owen was in there getting ready for work. After opening my bowels the contractions soon started, but I didn't know if it was contractions, so I told Owen to go to work.

He was having a go at me because I didn't know if I was in labour or not. He must have decided I was as he didn't go to work.

I phoned the doctor at the surgery, but he was not in yet. He phoned back and wanted to speak to me, but I couldn't because the contractions were coming thick and fast. He told Owen to time them and go to the hospital when they were less than five minutes, which they already were, so off we went. It was about a twenty-minute drive to the hospital, and when we got to some temporary traffic lights, he asked me if I wanted him to go through and I said, 'I don't care, just get me there'.

At the hospital I refused to go in the lift, as I was too frightened of getting stuck in there. I had to stop several times trying to climb the stairs. We were put into a labour room. The rooms were fairly new then, done out like hotel rooms, and I started stripping off, not caring that there were workmen working on a flat roof, but the midwife closed the curtains.

After examining me, she announced that I was 8cm dilated and would have the baby in half an hour. They gave me gas and air, but the first puff made me dizzy. That was taken off me and they gave me oxygen for the baby's sake as it was a quick birth. I was thinking, sod the baby.

Our community midwives had told us that we would get the urge to push, but I never did, so I started to push as though I was having a wee, but no, it's pushing as though you are having a poo! It was so painful that I kept letting the contractions ride, but I finally pushed the baby out with one almighty scream. Owen says he nearly fainted at that point.

Our son was born at 11:04 on Thursday 15th February 1990. They had to break my waters and cut me. I had to wait an hour for my doctor to finish surgery and come to stitch me up so that he could claim to have delivered the baby and get a fee for it! Again, being new to this we only found out afterwards. Rachael, the midwife, delivered him.

I was finally allowed to have a shower, and I never thought I'd get out with all the blood and gunge pouring out of me. My bum was black and blue, and I had to have heat treatment. Owen said bitterly afterwards 'You would have sent me to work and made me miss my son's birth!' Did he think I'd told him to go to work with that intention?

Owen's family visited that evening. Our son was jaundiced and had to have treatment in the special baby unit, though he seemed too big to be in there. I wanted to breast-feed him but he kept giving up, so we settled for the bottle and the midwives kept telling me that I had great nipples.

We could not agree on a name. I wanted John or Wayne, but Owen was keen on Daffydd. As I told him, I can't spell it, let alone say it! The only name we could agree on was Alun and to please Tony, Anthony as a middle name.

CHAPTER FIVE

MOTHERHOOD

Back in 1985/6 the BBC 'That's Life' programme with Esther Rantzen covered the subject of child abuse and consequently Esther set up the charity Childline. I was very moved by the programme and sent off my story, but soon realised that I had got off lightly compared to some of the stories that were read out. They encouraged everyone to 'confront your abuser'. I just did not have the guts to stand up to my dad, so I wrote to my mother and told her I did not want to see him again. She confronted him and he actually admitted it to her. She said we should meet to talk, and we met at a service station at the end of the M4. Not a lot was said. She told me he admitted to it but tried to blame me for it. She even said, 'Well, you never had any boyfriends'. What had that got to do with it? I was 11 when it started, not really into boys then and would it have made a difference? My mother was in another world!

Several times over the years, whenever the subject came up, she always said 'He was never like that!' In denial again. Mum and I used to meet up now and again and I even went to their, house but I could never relax and was anxious to get away early in case he returned early.

I'm not sure if it was me or Owen who told my mum that I had had a boy. I can remember asking Owen to tell friends of mine, John and Dorothy Young and I had to ask his brother Sam to do it as Owen kept 'forgetting'. I'm sure he didn't like me to have friends.

I did phone my mum to find out if she was coming to see the baby, and Dad answered the phone. I was told she was out, and when I said about her coming down he said, 'We both are, I have a right to see my grandson'. Again I just didn't have it in me to tell him where to go, or even point out that he had waived the right once he had touched me. So they turned up on the Saturday, and he walked in and congratulated Owen, looked at the baby but completely ignored me! He soon made the excuse of needing a fag to leave.

I don't know how it came about, but they would visit us and I started visiting them again. The subject of the abuse was never spoken of. Occasionally Owen would come with me, and he took over the role of bathing Alun. That annoyed me, as he did sod all at home. I can remember trips to the Cotswold Wildlife Park and a bird sanctuary. Alun was not a typical boy, not really into danger, and I can remember Dad saying 'He will have to spend some time with us to toughen him up'. Again I stayed silent, but I thought over my dead body. I'd have gone to court to prevent that if necessary. Not that I thought he would sexually abuse Alun, being a boy.

I was not a natural maternal mum. I found the routine of bottles, nappies and shoe-lace tying very tedious. Alun never slept for long. Once I left him screaming to get an hour's sleep, and woke with a start to realise he was still screaming. I thought someone would call in Social Services. I asked for help and attended meetings for advice, where they suggested no eye contact, go in, lay him down, walk out, leave it five minutes, then repeat, increasing the time you leave him, but Owen wouldn't have it. I'm not sure if he was concerned for Alun or for himself. He wouldn't come to the sleep clinic with me - he just didn't want to know. Even the woman at the clinic asked me if Alun was his! I thought she was having a go at me, suggesting I'd slept around, but maybe she thought he was not cooperating as she thought he didn't care for the boy if he wasn't the dad.

When I was first changing nappies, it felt like I was abusing him, but I'd give myself a shake and tell myself I'd be abusing him if I left him in the dirty nappy!

I wanted to get a part-time job. Sam and Gail had moved from London, bought a pub nearby and had a daughter. Ellie had practically brought up Ann while Sam and Gail ran the pub, but she would not have Alun for me for a few hours a day. She used to have him on a Tuesday when it was convenient for her. Once when she picked him up I saw that pleading look in Alun's eyes, the look I would have given my mother being left in my father's care. I refused to let him go again, which upset Ellie and the rest of the family, but I couldn't explain my reasons for it.

I was not keen to have another child but didn't want Alun to be an only child. Ann now had a sister, Laura, so I suggested to Owen that we tried for another baby and he agreed. Again it didn't take long for me to get pregnant, but this pregnancy was totally different. I was fine each morning until about 10 am and then for most of the rest of the day, I felt really ill. With a toddler this was hard work, as I just wanted to lie down and die.

We decided to wait to the twelve weeks before telling anyone. The scans were done around 15/16 weeks and we duly turned up. I can remember the midwife filling in forms, taking my blood pressure and asking routine questions, one of which was 'you did do a pregnancy test?' 'No' was my reply. We were trying, my periods stopped, and I felt ill for the first three months, so why waste a tenner on a kit? I think she thought either that I would not be pregnant or it would be a phantom pregnancy.

With Alun, the father was invited in for the scan, but this time they wanted to do the scan first. I'm not sure if protocol had changed or because they suspected that my womb would be empty. The radiographer seemed to be interested in two areas of my stomach, left and right. I strained to see the screen, and my first thought was, something is horribly wrong, the baby has split in two!

I turned to look at the radiographer, and she was grinning. It took a while for the penny to drop.

'It's not twins is it?' I asked.

'Oh can you tell?' she replied.

My mind started whirling. Alun still was not sleeping through the night. How was I going to cope with twins?

They said Owen could come in and asked me if I'd like to tell him. I said I would, but by the time he came in I was sobbing. God knows what he thought! Then the midwife said 'Your wife has had a shock, it's twins'.

We were left to wait outside to see the gynaecologist, and I was still shaking, thinking, why me? I'm not coping with one child, I'm being punished again. I vaguely remember them saying that I would be given a number of scans, as they like to keep an eye on twins because one sometimes pinches all the nutrients from the other, but it was all a blur to me.

Of course Owen wanted to stop off at his parents on the way home to tell them the 'good news'. I asked for a glass of water, and Tony could see I was really upset and followed me through to the kitchen, probably thinking something was seriously wrong. I told him and said, 'I can't cope with twins!' Then we went through to tell Ellie, and of course she was delighted and making promises to help out. Yeah, I thought, on your terms.

It was that evening that I had to go to the Fishguard Bay Hotel for a celebratory drink. The rest of The Thomases had not been told. I can't imagine how Ellie kept it quiet, so perhaps they were acting surprised. Owen said something like 'I want to raise a toast to the new baby and the baby's new brother or sister'. It was Gail that clicked first and shouted 'It's twins!'

Everyone was pleased except me. When I was pregnant with Alun I craved the attention, but now I was getting it and didn't want it. Gail had even joked about twins being in her family, and you can put a bet on yourself before the first scan, but it was too late for that. The local midwives had twins too and paid me a lot of attention. They asked if it was all right to inform the other mums who were expecting around the same time as me. I felt sorry for them and embarrassed that I was the favourite with the midwives.

The pregnancy went well, and I only put on half a stone more than with my first pregnancy. People didn't believe me when I said it was twins, as they didn't think I was big enough. The scans showed them doing well, more or less the same size but both in the breech position. The obstetrician told me he would not like to deliver one breech and certainly not two, so they decided to give me a planned caesarean section. The twins were due on the 19th June 1993 and they only did caesareans on Mondays unless it was an emergency, meaning it was a choice of the 14th or the 21st, and of course I could have gone into labour before the 21st, so the date was set for the 14th. The midwives told me that with twins the woman often went into labour up to five weeks before.

I went into hospital the night before and was put into a private side ward. The sister had a job to find both heartbeats, and I found out later that one baby had turned, so perhaps I could have delivered them myself.

We were left waiting all morning, and I thought because it was planned that I would be awake for it, they had me down to be put under. I insisted on staying awake, saying I would always wonder if they were mine if I wasn't there to see them being born. Owen had strict instructions to make sure the babies had their tags on before they came out of the room. They agreed to give me an epidural, and I had to lie on my side and get my knees on my chest. Excuse me, but I have this huge lump preventing me from doing this! I did my best, only for the anaesthetist to put his arm under my legs and shove my knees up further. I was lying on one of those plastic hospital beds and he burned the skin on my hip shoving me. Hours after the spine blocker had worked, I could still feel that burn.

I was taken into the operating theatre, where they positioned a screen so that I could not see what was going on. I'd have been fascinated to see. Owen came in all gowned up, I hardly recognised him. I remember hearing someone say, 'As it's twins we will do it this way'. Only afterwards I found out that instead of a neat scar along the pubic hair line I had been sliced straight up almost to my navel. I should have sued! Still to this day I am unable to wear bikinis.

I think it was the anaesthetist who kept cracking jokes. The surgeon had to ask him to stop as he couldn't clip me together because my tummy was wobbling with laughter. 'Here's the first one... a girl', he said, pulling her out by the ankles. I strained to see as they took her to be checked over and weighed - 5lb 9oz. Two minutes later another girl, slightly bigger at 5lb 13oz. They were soon given the all-clear and I was wheeled back into my side ward.

Again I tried to breast feed without much luck. On examining the first baby she had a fit, and they took her into special care for tests. I later learned that her fit was because that valve in the oesophagus that stops food coming back up was not fully formed, so milk would come back up into her nasal cavities and she would freeze and then struggle to breathe. Anyone would thrash about! I don't think they believed me, and it's still on her record as fits.

This time when the Thomas family visited, they found me with just the one baby and only close family were allowed into the special baby care unit. Sam picked up the other one and very nearly dropped her. Quick as a flash I said, 'It's OK Sam, I've got another one'. I thought it was funny.

That night I had the shivers and asked for another blanket,

and this was noted. Hospitals are known for being very hot, which must give germs ideal conditions. A day or two later, after getting the feeling back and getting out of bed, I was allowed onto a normal ward, four beds in a ward, where I hoped to meet other mums. Here a nurse took the catheter out, which was very painful, I still cringe at the memory.

I had only been there a few hours when I noticed that I had a few spots, which I suspected was chicken pox. Alun had had it a few weeks before. Although our mother used to mix us with kids that had it, we never caught it as children. I was put back in the side ward, and I can remember getting a right telling off for getting out to watch the Sea King helicopter land. I got a right row, for putting the other mother's at risk. They admitted that they didn't know the effects of chicken pox on newborn babies, so my girls were taken into special care and I was installed in the relatives' flat. They expected me to stay there while the girls had ten days of antibiotics. I felt as if I was in prison. They even had to get volunteer staff in who had had chicken pox. The window only opened a few inches, which didn't help, and of course I was not allowed out. So I insisted on going home, where I had a week to recover before the girls came home. I still felt very guilty and it's on my records that I did not bond with the girls.

We had agreed that if one was a girl we would call her Mia – this was suggested by Ellie and we both liked it, so the firstborn got the name. Again we could not agree on the other name. Owen liked Angharad, but I was not keen as he fancied someone by that name. However we gave it to Mia as her middle name. He also liked Helen, but a colleague of his had named her daughter Helen a few weeks before. I liked Susan and Gemma, but there was a Gemma in our street already. We settled for Emily, but we didn't have a clue about the middle name and I even asked the family to come up with a name that went with Emily. In desperation I registered her as Emily Louise at the six-week deadline.

The night I went into hospital, Alun slept through. I thought it must have been a fluke, but from then on he slept fine. It must have been something emotional or psychological, but what I'll never know. Alun never crawled - he bum-shuffled, which reminded me of a thalidomide child, and didn't walk till he was 19 months. He was still in nappies at three. Mia was quicker than Emily; they walked at 11 and 13 months. They amused themselves, and if it was quiet, you could be sure they were getting up to some mischief. They were a delight compared to having a single child.

Shortly after they came home, I bathed them and left Emily on the changing mat in the bathroom. Being a newborn she was perfectly safe as she wasn't going anywhere. I brought Mia down to feed her. Then Alun, now almost three and a half, came down the stairs carrying what appeared to be a doll, but then I knew we didn't have any dolls yet.

'Here you are Mum, I have brought you the other baby' he said. I think it was still some moments before I reacted. The thought that he could have dropped her or even fallen down the stairs with her! I tried to tell him he must never do that again and he burst into tears - of course he thought he was just helping.

He got on really well with his sisters, and in later years he would choose which sister he would play with, upsetting the other one.

Because Mia was a breech birth, they insisted that she went to have her hips checked. I didn't think it was necessary as she hadn't passed through my pelvis and I hadn't noticed any problems. I was sent an appointment, and Ellie looked after Alun and Emily while I took Mia to the hospital. We had a fair wait. The doctor was a short man and had the attitude to go with it. When it was our turn he asked me why I was there. I may have answered 'I was wondering the same'. He went on to rant, saying 'This is my adult clinic, I see children on such and such a day'. I explained that I had just received this appointment in the post, and did not know it was an adult clinic. He did seem to calm down after that, but there was no need for it.

He examined Mia and I hated to see that action they do with their legs to test the hips, which made her cry. He said he couldn't see anything wrong but wanted to see her in six months. I wrote to the hospital cancelling the appointment and pointed out that I was not going to subject my daughter to that rude little man!

To get away from the constant nappy-changing, and craving adult company, I volunteered to become a Special Constable. I spent an induction weekend at Carmarthen police headquarters. I went out one evening a week, but I was useless at it, not having any people skills. I did enjoy the company of adults. One copper I really remembered was Hywel, who started off as a Special and was also a part-time vicar. I suppose I had a crush on him and I think it was mutual. There were rumours that he had affairs. I've since got back in touch with him via Facebook, but I don't fancy him any more. Nothing happened when I was on duty. My neighbour was having his van vandalised and they did a stake out in our house, but of course it was all quiet that night. I expect it was someone in the street.

We went to a police ball, and Haverfordwest covered for them that night. Owen told me he had heard one of them say that I was the best-looking female officer they had, but then there were only a few.

One of the coppers was killed in a car accident and a detective committed suicide, with a hosepipe in the car. I really liked him, he used to give me lifts when I was hitching to have driving lessons. He was a Hancock, like the comic.

I saw my first dead body, a sudden death in a pub. The copper with me said I didn't have to go in, but I didn't know what all the fuss was about, it just looked like he was asleep.

When Alun was a baby I joined the Pembrokeshire Advanced Motorists, affiliated to the IAM. Willie Williams phoned me when Alun was yelling his head off so it was difficult to have a conversation, but I agreed to go to my first meeting at Haverfordwest Aerodrome. Willie had watched me turn up in our Astra GTE B reg and had already decided that I could drive. A Police A1 driver did a talk, and I asked how long would it take to pass the advanced test. He suggested six months, but said that of course it could take you longer.

I started having assessed runs with a woman, can't remember her name, it was all voluntary and after a few runs she decided for personal reasons she could no longer take me, so I was passed over to a sergeant, think his name was Arthur. I can remember once approaching a bend too fast because I thought the road went straight on, though in fact it was just a farm road. I skidded to a stop. He told me I should have accelerated into the bend, because acceleration gives grip to the front wheels. It's something I have never forgotten and it has got me out of trouble a few times.

He told me I was ready for my test, but I said I didn't have the nerve. He got annoyed with me then, probably thinking I had wasted his time, so I put in for it. The examiner was another officer, Lewis, a detective. I didn't drive my best but he passed me anyway.

I became an avid member of the local group. I became secretary and newsletter editor, though I can't type and I did find it quite stressful. I got a father and daughter through their test but could not get through to a postman how he should drive, so I passed him on to someone else and the guy gave up after that. He used to frighten me. I quickly realised that it's all about attitude. Some who think they are great drivers are in fact terrible, and others like myself who don't have confidence turn out to be considerate drivers – note I don't use the word 'good'.

Again Owen used to put me down when I was practising for my advanced test. It was the only thing I was good at, and he wanted to destroy that. After having the twins I found it too much and after the move I was just a member in name only.

It took me years to believe that I was a good driver, and I still think you can never stop learning. Every situation is different, and we all make mistakes. I have had a few compliments over the years, from my grandmother, who said I am the only one that she feels safe with, my son, who said 'My mum is the only good woman driver' and recently from a passenger. I have no idea who he was but he said 'You are the best bus driver I have come across'. With 'spy in the cab' and consistently being rated highly, maybe he is right.

I am hopeless on a racing track but I like to think that I am considerate to other road users, from the person pushing a buggy to the cyclist and horse rider. I have also had a go on a skidpan, and the instructor was convinced I'd done it before, but apart from the post van occasionally losing grip I'd never experienced a real skid. I read the theory and put it into practice.

When the girls were around four months old I had a falling out with our neighbour's daughter. The people at number four were having their house renovated and I came home one day to find a right mess in our yard. I had a go at their son-in-law who was up on the roof, as the danger to my kids was my concern. He did clear it up but obviously I could not let the kids out there with rubble falling on them.

Later that evening before Owen had come home, there was a knock at the door. The girls were sitting quite happily, and I left them to open the door. It was the neighbour's daughter. Before I knew what was happening, she had grabbed me, slammed my head into the door and punched me a few times. Alun had come through to the hall and was watching this. She ranted on about me having a go at her husband and accused me of not wanting her parents to have their house done up. I pointed out that this was not true as their house was the only one letting the street down. She said 'I won't hit you hit you again as your little boy is watching' but proceeded to do so anyway.

I called the station to report the assault, I did not know her name or address but told them it was the neighbour's daughter and thought her name was Debbie. They knew her anyway as she had form. She denied it and her husband said she was at home. The police said it was my word against hers, so I went knocking on a few doors hoping to find out if anyone had seen anything. My neighbour opposite said he hadn't but a friend of his was walking up the street, heard a commotion and saw her leave. He was quite happy to make a statement.

We had to attend an identity parade, when he picked her out. They did not bother to get me to pick her out. A court date was set for Cardigan, but I had never given evidence, and I was terrified. Just before we were expected to go in, the solicitor told us that at the last minute she had changed her plea to guilty. She received a fine and was told that if she came to court again she would be sent down.

When the girls had their first birthday, they had a cake in the shape of a pig. Emily pinched the tail off it as Owen walked in and everyone was singing 'Happy Birthday'. We moved into the back bedroom and split the main bedroom in two, but there was no room to swing a cat, so we put the house on the market.

It took a long time to sell and then the couple threatened to pull out if we couldn't complete a week early. We wanted to move to the Carmarthen area, Owen for work, while I wanted some distance from his family and to be a bit closer to mine. We settled for a place on the edge of a village between Whitland and Narberth, but neither of us was really happy with the purchase. It was two old stone cottages. The second was used as a workshop and did not have permission for residential use, but there was a large extension on the back with a large garden. It was close to a bend and the traffic used to whiz past.

Mum took the kids out while we were moving. When we turned up with the furniture the money had not been transferred, so the family did not want us to move in, but eventually they agreed that the furniture could come in. Thankfully it was sorted out. The kitchen was the best room, the kids' bedroom was above and the living room with our bedroom and bathroom above were in the old part of the house, with small poky windows, so was quite dark. Owen wanted to change the house's name to the Welsh version, but apparently there was one in the village, as we found out when he came round with some of our mail.

We enrolled Alun in the local school, which was Welsh speaking, but I don't think he liked it. I felt really sorry for him but I thought it was better to learn it when he was small. He was picked up every morning by minibus. I met a woman from the village, Kay Jones, who was really nice. Her son was four months younger than the girls and she had an older daughter, but I felt her husband didn't treat the daughter very well as she was not his. Kay and I used to go to exercise classes together and mother and toddlers.

My parents visited us once that summer, and Tony often popped in on his way home. Ellie complained about the 31-mile journey but used to come on shopping trips to Carmarthen.

When I started going to Asda in Carmarthen I didn't know they had twin trolleys so I got Alun to push one sister in one trolley while I had the other and did the shopping. He started to wander off and then we lost each other, and I was panicking. He tried to look for me in the car park, and by the time a member of staff stopped him he was in tears. They helped us transfer them to a double trolley. After that I waited until Owen was home to look after the kids before I went off to do the shop.

My mum turned fifty on the 1st October that year, 1994, and we went down for her birthday party. She enjoyed it and I did too. Owen as usual played the dad part, making out that he was very attentive, whereas at home I was left to get on with it. Afterwards he said 'I hope we don't have to do that again for a long time'. Christ, I thought, we are always at his parents and he can't be bothered to see mine once in a while.

He didn't get his wish, as the following Sunday he answered the phone to be told by one of my mum's neighbours that my father had died! When he told me, I thought he was joking. I thought the bastard would live to be a very old man, terrifying me for a long time to come. I can remember wandering round and round the garden for ages trying to get my head around it. Someone up there likes me after all, I was thinking. My daughters are safe from him.

Eventually I phoned my mum and she was in hysterics, so I promised to drive down. I arrived around ten that night, to find my brother and Uncle Bill there. Mum was talking as though Dad was still there. She said they had gone for a walk and he was having pains which he thought was indigestion. He said he just wanted to go home, and drank some lemonade to get him to belch. They both went to sleep on the sofas (they had one each) and he never woke up. He was only 55.

I stayed three days trying to sort things out, going through his papers. They had just bought a new car, and I found a signed piece of paper to cover the payments if anything happened to him, but he had not sent it off. It took months for his assets to be sorted as he did not have a will, but in the end Mum had the house paid for, paid off the car loan and was left with around ninety grand, which she invested, although she was always claiming poverty.

One thing that sticks in my mind about that time was answering the phone the following morning to a man who asked for my father. He said something like 'Where is the grumpy old git, slept in?'

I said, 'Has my uncle not phoned your office, he promised to do so? My father had a massive heart attack yesterday and died'.

The poor man at the other end of the line was stunned. I had to repeat it, and he asked how it had happened. I felt sorry for him, as he must have cursed himself for his big mouth, but later I found it funny and I think Mum did too.

She hardly slept that night, and I kept waking to hear her crying. Her doctor gave her some pills. The funeral was set for the following week. After Owen's attitude I didn't know if he would attend - he did, but chose to travel up later.

When I went with Mum and Vince to the chapel of rest, Vince would not come in. I didn't really want to see Dad in his coffin but I went for Mum's sake. The cold struck me but of course it needs to be cold. He was laid out in a suit, with a grin on his face, still laughing at me! Mum wanted me to touch him, but I didn't want to. I imagined him grabbing me like in horror films. But he was cold and stiff, so at least I knew he really was dead and not asleep.

A neighbour of Mum's looked after the kids while we went to the crematorium. I was really surprised at how many folk were there. I had expected just the family but there were many colleagues and all sorts of folks. I did wonder if some folk just attend funerals uninvited, like standing outside a church when someone is getting married! Only family came to the wake, but I would have liked to have seen the other people folk to ask them how they knew him.

About three weeks after the funeral, I did have a good cry. My cousin Jenny didn't attend the funeral, as she was teaching English in Spain. She sent a letter which her mum read out, saying 'Uncle Berwick was like a second dad to me'. All I could think of was, why could he not be a dad to me? I was not crying over his death but over a lost childhood and the father–daughter relationship I should have had.

Mum gradually got her life back together and now lives with another man, separate bedrooms, I think it's just for company. She sold the house, they bought a smaller one together and they now live in a luxury mobile home. They did have to evacuate once because of flooding, and he had not kept the insurance payments up so they had to finance it themselves. At least his brother is a plumber.

Owen started going quiet on me and I knew something was wrong. He was coming home later and later. The following Mother's Day I took the kids to my mum's and left him a note saying 'I feel like a single mother, I might as well be one'. He phoned me on the Sunday and claimed I'd hidden the letter, but it was clearly popped up on an otherwise empty table!

He said he agreed with me and we would talk when he got back. He didn't say much, apart from the fact that he had arranged to move in with a colleague.

CHAPTER SIX

SPLITTING UP

Owen and I made love for the last time, and I put all my effort into it, knowing I was saying goodbye. It was a horrible day when he left, 5th April 1995, and everything seemed to happen just before my birthday. I cried and cried. It felt like a part of me had died. His parents still asked me over for Easter that year, but I think they understood when I refused. I still cringe at the thought now.

I didn't know how I would cope, and it didn't help to receive a solicitor's letter asking me how I planned to pay the mortgage. The only income I had was my child benefit. My solicitor at first told me we could not divorce for two years, but then Owen admitted he was seeing a very pretty reporter from work. I stopped watching the news channel he filmed for and it took me years to watch that side again. It's bad enough when your husband is having an affair, but to see her face every time you turned on the news!

He claimed he hadn't started seeing her until we split. He would turn up wanting to take Alun out with her, and the girls would scream for their father, so I insisted he took them as well. They were under two and still a lot of work.

With this information I went back to the solicitor and cited for divorce on his adultery. I was very lonely and could not see how I would find anyone else with three kids. Computers were not internet linked then. I joined a dating site where you sent letters and they were forwarded to the person for a fee. I had a few dates with local men, but nothing came of it.

Then I wrote to someone in the Swansea area who said he was a part-time dad. We met at a disco they ran in Carmarthen and hit it off. He was another Owen, so at least it would be all right to talk in my sleep!

He was a shepherd, two years older than me and bald. He came over the next night and we had a meal. I had a local girl babysitting and she thought we had a prowler, so I found her mother there when we got back.

Owen stayed the night, but he was not very good in bed and I faked most of my orgasms. His kids came to stay at weekends and I had started making the second part of the house into a flat, as Mum had given me some money.

I thought I could get a lodger and have an income from that. A guy I employed was not very good and made a right mess of the patio area - Owen was not impressed. Owen's kids stayed in the flat, but after their mother found out, she insisted they slept in the house. They were really nice kids, Gary, Neil and Rachael.

Owen Two was taking a job in Hereford, and I used to visit him at the weekends when Owen One had our kids. I really enjoyed going around the sheep on the quad bike. He got a tied cottage and we moved in with him. Alun was happier in an

English school, but used to draw some really dark paintings. I would meet Owen One halfway on a Friday night with the kids and pick them up on a Sunday. His relationship with Janet only lasted four months. He came to an open evening at Alun's school and I thought he was coming onto me - too late, I was with the other Owen now.

Soon after that Owen One met Patricia, an Irish woman who shared the same birthday as his mother and was from the same town, Waterford, so they must have got on really well. The girls really took to her, but I think Alun was a bit restrained.

We had three moves within the estate farm cottages. The second one was set right off the main road with a garden, very quiet but too small, only two bedrooms, bad enough my three sharing but there were six when Owen Two's kids came. There were woods which you could walk through to the farm, and I often got lost, as I never had a good sense of direction. We would see deer quite often.

Something happened that still sticks in my mind which I am ashamed of and cringe at the thought of. Alun was at school and the girls were happily playing. I had had a bath and was drying my hair, and I thought it had gone quiet. I finally decided to check on the girls, and they had gone.

I panicked. Thankfully a neighbour had seen them walking hand-in-hand down the lane towards the main road. She gave me a right row, which I deserved. Owen put a lock on the garden gate after that.

I tried to take up netball again and joined the Hereford ladies, but never felt I fitted in. Instead I started coaching the girls at Alun's school. It took all the year groups to make up a five-a-side team. I don't think some of the mothers were impressed by my method of coaching. I was treating them the same as adults, but it produced results. They started off being slaughtered 23-0 but at a tournament they attended it was nearer 10-7. I enjoyed the coaching as much as playing.

On one of my trips to buy a netball, Owen and I filled in our details for a competition, not ever thinking we would hear anything. He won a two-week holiday to Australia, and we planned to go in the February. Owen was going to have the kids as usual and his parents would have them for the rest of the time.

On the Friday I travelled with the kids to meet him at the usual place. He was late, not unusual, but after about 40 minutes a woman popped out from the café to give me a message to say he wasn't coming. I thought he was trying to scupper our chances of this holiday. It turned out there had been a major disaster, a fire on a ship, anyway he was stuck on a cliff somewhere filming. He finally got back to me the next day, saying if you want to go get the kids to his parents. We had to take them all the way to Goodwick. Once there I would have liked to visit friends, but Owen was anxious to get back as his kids were needing a lift home too, so we popped in very briefly to see my ex-neighbour in Goodwick.

The flight to Australia was horrendous, twelve hours to Singapore, where we had to get off but for only forty minutes when they cleaned and refuelled, and then it was a further six and a half hours to Melbourne. Here we had several hours before our next flight, so we popped into Melbourne and went around a market. I wanted to buy presents for the kids – plenty of time for that, Owen pointed out.

Our next stop was Canberra, where we were met by a woman from their sports institute which had organised the competition. We were shown round and given a fitness test. Owen did better than me, not surprisingly, and she asked us if we would like some coaching. I wanted to but he didn't, so she arranged a day out for us instead.

The hotel was five star with everything laid on, and we were given vouchers for taxis. Our day out was to a national park with a local 'Grizzly Adams' type character. The parks were closed due to a ranger strike, so we didn't see anything. He made us some billy tea and recommended sugar but I found it too sweet!

Our next destination was Sydney, where we found ourselves in an apartment which was part of a hotel. The only thing laid on was breakfast in the form of small packets of cereal. It was a let-down after Canberra. The Mardi Gras was on and there were gays walking down the street everywhere holding hands. It didn't bother me but Owen was very anti-gay. I often think that guys like that must be in denial.

We hired a car and I insisted on a manual, but the one they intended to give us had been hired out and they wanted to give us an upgrade which was an automatic. I opted for the smaller manual they had, as an automatic box takes the enjoyment out of driving, I told her, I think she thought I was mad as they all drive autos there. Owen had forgotten his licence so I had to drive. That worked well as I don't like navigating and he did.

We had a few trips out. I can remember going on one trip when we were warned not to touch the trees, which of course I did, and then rinsed my hands in the river. Something moved in the water - could have been crocodiles! The crocs we did see were in a park and I kept well behind the wall.

We missed our next flight to Cairns. We had arranged to drop the car off near the airport, but we got lost in a one-way system and then went to domestic flights, not realising it was an international flight. It was no problem getting transferred to another – can't imagine that here. So we did fly domestic. I had awful pain in my ears on landing.

This time we were in a complex, with nothing included. Breakfast was 11 Australian dollars, and the exchange at time was about four dollars to the pound. It was stifling there. The room had air-conditioning but as soon as you opened the door it hit you. There were crickets outside.

The complex had a pool and even Owen got in, though he didn't like swimming. Part of the prize was a diving lesson, and we went out to the barrier reef but neither of us took them up on the diving.

I persuaded Owen to go rafting but the wet season had not started and the trip was really tame, though we did see a platypus in the river. One night they had sixteen inches of rain, but we didn't mind getting caught in it as it was warm.

All too soon we were on our way home. We had left my car at Mum's in Swindon, and the brakes had stuck on. It was a white Volvo estate, the only car that would hold a double buggy and a load of shopping. On taking it to ATS we found it was going to cost a fortune to do the work required, so we part-exchanged it for a K reg Astra. Owen used to have a VW Polo which he got rid of and took out car finance to pay the rest on the Astra, so this was our car.

We were happy at this time, we even got engaged and were house hunting. I have always had lengthy periods, and after having Alun they lasted eleven days and after the twins it was a question of three weeks on and one off instead of the other way around. I was fed up with it, so I went to see the doctor to ask for the pill again. I'd stopped taking it years ago as I'd sussed that it gave me the migraines. In Wales a gynaecologist had put me on HRT, saying it wouldn't affect me, but every nine days I was having a migraine.

When I described my symptoms to the Hereford doctor, he said he could not legally give me the pill. It was only on reading a feature in a magazine that I found out that I could be in danger of having a stroke. I told him that if he could offer me a hysterectomy I'd have it tomorrow. With that attitude, he said, and the fact that you have three children, you can have one.

I was due to go in to Hereford General on a Monday, but a few days before Alun fell off a swing in the care of a neighbour and broke his wrist badly. Joshline, who was looking after him, was really upset, but I told her that accidents happen. Alun wanted his dad, so he came up and spent the night with him at the hospital.

Owen was also due to have his kids for the weekend. He'd been minding my girls and his wife was threatening him, saying that if he didn't come to get his kids, she wouldn't let him have them again. She was doing this all the time, and kept telling him to get something sorted via a solicitor.

Alun had to have his wrist operated on and their dad took all three kids home while I was in hospital. My womb was sucked out, the bleeding stopped completely and I think physically it's the best thing I have ever done. I enjoyed my weekends free from having any children, but Owen was the opposite and would have had them all, all the time. I tried to plan for one weekend with the kids and one without, but every time it was arranged like that Owen's wife would change it around, so I'd change it again and she would change it back. It was wearing me down.

Things were starting to go wrong between us, and I think I knew it was really going downhill, when we went into town one day and Owen wanted to see an insurance broker to arrange life insurance. He took out £150,000 worth, naming his kids as benefactors, turned to me and said 'you will have to sort yourself out'. I admired him for protecting his kids, but he really had given me a kick in the stomach. I think the broker saw this too.

My mind was reeling after this and I went quiet. He asked me what was wrong, and I thought, as if you don't know. I could imagine myself ending up in a woman's hostel with the kids, and was imagining grotty rooms and a load of butch lesbian women, tons of nosy kids, shared facilities. So I made the decision to send the kids to live with their dad. He could not take them until September.

Meanwhile I'd been enquiring about jobs and got some work driving for a private car hire firm in Hereford called Tim's. On Sunday August 31 1997 we woke up to the news of Lady Diana's death in a car crash. I was due to take a Chinese lad to a private school near Colchester that day, and he hardly spoke a word of English. I hated having to navigate and got lost several times, but eventually got him there.

On the way back I found myself going through Leeds – I don't think the boss would have been impressed by the mileage on the car.

At one time I was allowed to take a car home and misjudged going into our drive, damaging the bumper. I would have paid the £37 repair myself if I could have afforded it.

I picked some guy up from Birmingham Airport, who had come home just for the weekend from Germany. I think he expected me to drive really fast and kept slagging me off, saying things liked I drove like his grandmother. I'm sure I said I was not risking my licence for his benefit, but that didn't stop him. I refused to drive him again and I wouldn't be surprised if he said 'Don't send me her again'.

We also used to pick up mentally disabled kids. One used to grab hold of a handful of the driver's hair. They tried to send a driver with a number one haircut, but it was not always possible.

The job did not pay very well, as you only got paid for actual drives. I was looking every week for something else and got a job as a poultry assistant at a broiler farm, thirteen miles from where I lived. It consisted of walking the sheds every day, picking up the dead birds, making sure the feed and water was working and weighing birds. It was very smelly, hard work and quite physical, especially when we did 'turnovers'. They would come in as day-old chicks and would be killed at around nine weeks.

Guy, the bloke I worked with, was nice and quiet, but one day he didn't turn up. I never found out what the problem was, but he never returned. Paul, the boss, took on the role for a bit. I think he considered himself middle working class, sending his three sons to private schools. He had a Rottweiler dog which didn't take a liking to me, but he wouldn't believe she would go for anyone until he saw her going for me.

He advertised Guy's job and took on a young man of about

23. He seemed OK at first, but I upset him by saying something one day and he told me to go home. I was stunned, and didn't know if he was serious. Even Jean could not believe it.

I carried on for a bit, then went to see Paul. Peter had already spoken to him and told me to go home but come back tomorrow. Even Owen was annoyed by that. Peter turned out to be a bit of a prat. He'd damaged a van on ice, blaming the tyres, and then wrote off the van by driving it along a flooded road. He also started not turning up for work and eventually was let go, and then it was me and Paul again.

Now I was having the kids every other weekend and of course we had Owen's kids too, but not having any during the week, I didn't mind any more.

Owen and his sons were into football and rugby. I did once go to a match with him but I found it embarrassing, all these folks jumping up and down every time their side got the ball. I was the only one not doing it. I have never been one to go with the flow, which is probably why I'm not a smoker.

With having the six kids at the weekend we found ourselves doing things separately. For a while we shared the car so we could not take the kids together. We were drifting apart.

We went to the Royal Welsh Show every year. Owen's brother Mike was at one time the Welsh shearing champion, and a lot of time was spent watching him, but once you have seen a few sheared it gets boring, so I used to wander around the stalls.

Mike once came to help out at lambing – there were around 1300 ewes and they did it in two lots. Someone had to be on hand all the time. It was a tiring time and Owen had a small caravan in the sheds so he could get a bite to eat and even some sleep. The farm manager's son and I witnessed Mike bashing hell out of an ewe that had sat on her triplets, smothering them - he was thumping and kicking her. She did not understand what she'd done, and in my opinion the stall was too small for a ewe with triplets.

For the last lambing I was there, in April 1999, Owen had a New Zealander female lamber to help. She was questioning me about him all the time! He started spending more and more time in the caravan while I was back at the cottage with my three. I'll never know for sure if they were up to anything, but she sheared his hair, which I used to do, and he always took his shirt off for that.

One time when I was bringing in washing she came back to the cottage to watch football with him, and I made a remark about not waiting until I'd gone, as she was really rubbing my nose in it. She walked off and he took her back to the farm. Then he came back, shot up the stairs and said to me 'Why don't you just fuck off?'

This was seen by Alun, who never forgot it and said he didn't like Owen after that. I was going to take my furniture to my mum's. She said she was going to put it in her garage, but I'd managed to get a room in a stables house and she had room to store my stuff. The house was filthy, there was no lock on my door and I knew her twelve-year-old daughter was looking through my stuff, eating my food, using my vacuum cleaner to suck up straw and my things were getting broken. I was thinking she'd just throw me out, but I found it difficult to complain. When I'd split from Owen Two, I'd left him enough pots and pans, plates etc. He bought some stuff off me and gloated when

I'd added it up wrong, as he'd saved himself a tenner! But when I pointed out that the car was a third mine he slammed the notepad down and went off on one, and I as usual gave in. I always ended up losing out on my relationship breakdowns. His kids obviously took his side. I think I was closer to Neil but I can remember being in floods of tears watching them go off somewhere, Neil looked up at the window, I'm not sure if he was gloating at me or felt sympathy but I ducked down anyway.

On the day I was moving out, Owen did ask me what my plans were as he still thought I was taking my stuff to my mum's. I snapped something like 'I'm going aren't I, what's it got to do with you?' Maybe there was some regret on his part.

Years later I cut him out of the photos of him with my kids, but there were a few nice ones, especially one of Neil, which I sent to his grandfather without my address. I don't have any ill feelings for Owen now. He was just trying to do the best for his kids and I expect he is a very happy grandfather by now.

Friends of mine had helped me move there. Gini and I used to go to a private pool once a week and became good friends. They introduced me to Roger Arnold, who had the gift of the gab. I was enthralled by a story he told about his wife's funeral. I now know it was his party piece. His wife had died in a car accident – they're called 'collisions' now, for good reason. She was overtaking a vehicle and hit a lorry head on. They had a five-year-old boy. Friends had looked after him and he came back to Roger's after the funeral. That night neither could sleep, Jake came in with Roger and Roger ended up in Jake's bed. Jake came running through to him saying 'I've got a secret'. Roger got him to tell. He's supposed to have said he'd seen mummy in a bubble. She had come through the window, told him she loved them, and the bubble disappeared behind a tree. Behind that tree was the car she had the accident in!

Jake could not remember that story, so whether there was anything to it or maybe he dreamt it, I'll never know, but every time Roger was in a crowd this story would be told, I got to hear it many times. He always told people that Jane was his first wife when in fact she was his second. He had a daughter by his first wife, about ten years younger than me, and when I met him he had a third wife whom he'd split from. I called her Psycho Sue.

Roger and I started seeing each other. At first he kept me a secret from his friends and family. I was so desperate being in this grotty place and having a grotty job. I could not see a way out, I'd never lived on my own and just could not see myself coping. We very quickly started a relationship, but Gini was not impressed with this and went off me. Roger was doing their milking, but soon stopped turning up. He drank three quarters of a bottle of brandy a night to get himself to sleep. He started asking to borrow money off me, and I ended up paying his domestic bills.

My landlady went away and left some ex-army guy in charge. He told me that if I was not back by 10pm the door would be locked. I was having my kids that weekend. I collected them and left the kids in the car while I collected some clothes, giving Alun instructions that if I wasn't back soon he should call the police, but the ex-soldier had guests and was nice as pie. We spent the weekend dossing at Roger's.

I soon moved in with him. I should have hung out, as it was shortly after this that I was offered housing, a flat near

Leominster. Roger told me it was a horrible estate, so I turned it down, but that could have been a ploy. Now I know I should have taken my chances.

That summer my Uncle Ray died. It was a hot summer and his body was not discovered for two weeks. Roger was going to come to the funeral with me, but Mum didn't think it was appropriate. At the funeral the vicar asked if anyone wanted to speak, but no one did. I half expected his daughter to stand up and say what she thought of him. Their mother had MS and they had seen their dad throwing her down the stairs. They divorced and my uncle remarried and had another son. That marriage had also broken down, and neither his second wife or son attended the funeral.

Roger had a load of unopened bills. I'm not sure if I opened one or it had been opened, but I found out that he owed £7,000 for boarding school fees for Jake and they were not going to let him back until the debt was cleared. So Roger was also looking for a way out, and that came in the form of me. I'd still not had my divorce settlement from Owen and Roger talked me into house-hunting with him. He was also expecting money from the sale of his and Sue's house. I wanted to move back to Wales so that I could see the kids more. We spent several weekends looking, and I even had to feign being sick so that we could go house-hunting. We just could not quiet afford anything.

Roger, browsing in a farming magazine, suggested Scotland, and pointed out a few, one in particular on a Scottish island in the Orkney Islands, so we drove up to see it. We looked at one near Thurso but you couldn't go outside because of the midges!

The house was really nice. It had only one bedroom but it

had two living rooms which could be doubled up to a bedroom. My main concern was seeing the kids. Roger said they could come back to live with us and he had a friend who had a helicopter, and he would fly them up. So with a heavy heart I agreed to buy this croft with him.

I met Jake and he did not take to me at all, I think because Sue spoiled him rotten and he realised that he was not going to get away with things with me. In fact, like father like son, Jake was planning his own scheme. Roger with his big mouth kept saying to my three that they could live with us in Scotland, and I knew this would go back to their father. Roger spent a lot of time with Sue, as he said he had to sort things out. She had a key to his house and one time we were away, she'd let herself in after seeing a pair of my shoes and took some photos of me and my kids. I threatened to get the police onto her. After that she burst in one night, having a go at him for seeing me. He told me to go upstairs and she told me to come down if I dared. I don't like confrontation but I saw red. I came down, giving as good as I got, and she backed out of the door. Later she came back with her sister. My nerve had gone then, so I called the police, but by the time they had arrived, she had left and Roger was back. He just fobbed the policeman off and would not give him Sue's address. She didn't want Roger but she didn't want anyone else to have him.

Even the night before our move, he spent the early hours with her, not knowing if it was the right thing to do, but it was too late now, as under Scottish law you have to pay a percentage if you back out. Jake had spent that last weekend with his mother's family to say goodbye, but Roger had received a call from his brother-in-law, who told him 'You are not taking the boy to Scotland!'

I don't think Roger had even told them of our plans, but of course Jake had told them and said he didn't want to go. I was all for going to get him. Roger said to leave it as they would soon get fed up with him and no longer want him. With Jake's mother dying I really felt for the boy and naively thought he just needed a stable home, not to be pushed from pillar to post, so we left without him.

I was so cheesed off with the poultry job that I only gave him a week's notice. I'd been on several poultry courses and he refused to give me my certificates. Roger didn't have much furniture, and we collected my stuff from the stables on the way, though we had to leave some stuff. A friend of Roger's was driving the long-wheelbase van and we travelled in my car. I had bought a Metro that kept breaking down. Roger got me to take out a loan to buy a Peugeot. I have no idea how I was to keep up the payments on the loan for the car without an income.

It rained heavily on the way up. I had bought new wiper blades for my car, but Roger had not fitted them properly and one came off on the motorway. We kept on going and the windscreen was badly scratched. Roger didn't even want to stop to get a new one, as though he was running away from something. We also nearly ran out of diesel on the way as the car had a faulty fuel gauge, but fortunately I had a spare gallon in the boot.

After a long drive, with two expensive ferry crossings, we arrived at our new home on the small island. Pat, the seller, was there to greet us with lunch and then she was picked up to get the evening ferry. She just took a suitcase, leaving all their furniture. We sold a lot of it, preferring to use our own. It was 1st October 1999, my mum's birthday, but she was on holiday anyway.

We brought with us two Labradors, mother and son. The son was supposed to be Jake's dog, bought for him on a promise, and the owner said he would be putting his mother Bonnie down as she was too old to have any more puppies, so we bought her too.

We soon had to take a trip into town to sign on and take the dogs to the vets. The cheaper option was to have Sam done rather than get Bonnie spayed. We took a trip to register with a doctor, and I took Roger in with me as we had been told that she was a tyrant and a celibate lesbian who liked nothing better than to do internals. I was terrified of her. I went to see her to get my ears syringed and after I sat down and said what was wrong, she asked why I was there. I repeated myself and she asked again why was I there. I admitted that I didn't understand. She said. 'Why are you here in my evening surgery when it is reserved for emergencies and those that work?' I hadn't known that!

She did my ears, but made a right fuss as I had not bought my own towels! NHS cutbacks? Roger of course charmed her and could even cuddle her. Roger, I learned, was a hypochondriac. Over the six-plus years we were together he'd told me several times that he was dying of cancer, always a different one. I'd never make a nursemaid and not very good at sympathy either. Instead of getting his ears syringed he stuck a needle in his ear and brought out a long lump of wax.

We had only been on the island a month when I received a solicitor's letter. As I opened it I began to shake. It was from

Owen's solicitor, saying that as I'd abandoned my children they presumed I would not object to him having residency of them. These letters always came on a Saturday when you can't get hold of anyone. I knew it was Roger opening his big mouth that Owen had got in there first.

I think Roger did phone our Scottish solicitor at home, but he could only advise me to get one back in England or Wales as he couldn't act for me. It was a long weekend. Come Monday I got a solicitor from Haverfordwest who was from Fishguard and we vaguely knew each other, but her name escapes me now. She took the details. I had to send the letter to her and soon bought a fax machine, which had plenty of use. I received a date in February to see the court welfare officer.

It was a long winter. The hydro went off twice, for 36 hours each time, until a helicopter could trace where the fault lay. I wanted to go out for the Millennium celebrations, but Roger didn't so we stayed in. Maybe just as well as there was a domestic at the hall – a husband stabbed his wife in the breast and the police were involved.

We found out on New Year's Day that it's traditional in Orkney to call on folk armed with booze, and as there were no resident police, folk drank and drove, often ending up in a ditch. If you passed a seemingly driverless car it was usually a kid driving it.

The following Christmas Eve, we were invited to a party hosted by neighbours, a mile up the road, and it was a good do. The weather was really rough and ended up a blizzard. On the way home we ran out of diesel and had to walk the last mile. Of course I got the blame for not putting diesel in the vehicle.

Roger was only wearing a shirt, though I'd had the sense to bring a coat. I left him ranting, intending to try to siphon some diesel from the lorry.

Roger turned up when I was attempting this. He started to rant about how useless I was and said he wanted me out, but I reminded him that it was half my house.

Next morning we were woken by the council roadman, who was clearing the road of snow. Our vehicle was blocking the single-track road and I could not rouse Roger to get up, too much drink at the party. When he finally woke up we took the lorry to tow the car back. It was still snowing hard. I was expected to tow in reverse the mile home. Not licensed to drive the lorry, I kept having to stop to clear the snow off the mirrors while Roger was ranting, but I could not hear him with the wind.

Eventually he lost his patience and we swapped places. All this time he was telling me how useless I was and saying he wanted me out, he'd had enough.

That Christmas Day we were invited out for dinner. On telling the story Roger just laughed it off, not displaying any of his aggression in front of them.

February dawned and Roger got Dan, who had driven our furniture van up, to come up to get me. I travelled down with him on Valentine's Day, the 14th. Several times we tried to phone Roger and the phone was constantly engaged to the point where we thought there must be a fault. It turned out he had spent over six hours on the phone to Sue in two lots. The phone was in my name and when I asked him about it after getting this huge bill, his answer was, 'I didn't know if you were coming back'! Where would I go? It dawned on me that he was already keeping her sweet in case I didn't!

I stayed with my mum and borrowed her car to go to Carmarthen. I was ushered into one room and Owen and the kids were in another – I felt like a criminal. The welfare officer interviewed us both. Owen was put in his place when he tried to say I'd abandoned them. The welfare officer pointed out that I was there, so that was not the case. I never could put myself over very well and as usual ended up getting upset. He also spoke to Alun, but considered the girls too young. The kids were brought in and they were all over me, tears all round, clinging to me for dear life.

The welfare officer was satisfied that I was not a threat to them so I was allowed to take them to the park for an hour. We stopped at a paper shop to get some sweets, and I can remember the woman saying 'not at school?' I think I just stuttered 'No'. how do you explain they have permission to be off school and why? It was none of her business anyway.

We sat in the park, but none of the kids wanted to leave me to play. Trying not to break down again, I asked the kids where they wanted to live. Emily opted for with me, Mia wanted to live with their grandparents Tony and Ellie and I thought Alun said with his dad. I knew I had lost, as they would not split them up and Tony and Ellie's was not an option. The girls' opinion did not count anyway. So when we returned to the welfare office, which was also the probation office, not the sort of place to bring children, I told the officer I would be withdrawing my claim as Alun had decided he wanted to live with his dad. At this point Alun burst out 'I did not say that Mum'!

I was horrified. I could have sworn that was what he'd said. Alun was in tears now and repeated he'd not said that. Owen was brought in giving me looks that could kill, I'd upset HIS children again. The officer had a chat with Alun and concluded that Alun was trying to please us both when it should be the other way around.

My friend Kay had agreed to let us stay a few days with the kids, and Owen reluctantly dropped them off later. We had a nice few days; it was so good of Kay to give us refuge. When Owen came to collect them Emily clung to me and had to be peeled off finger by finger, and I had to tell her, you have to go back or they won't let you come for Easter. It was agreed that I could have them for two weeks in the holidays, but he still wanted them for Christmas, so they were to have an extra week off in January from school to be with me then.

Dan again took me home. Now the problem was how to raise the money to get them up three times a year. Owen of course would not help - he would not even let me have the child benefit for those few weeks. I put a notice in the only shop on the island, asking for help in raising the £3,000 a year it would cost me to have my children up in the holidays, giving copies of references.

In May 2000 I got a few mornings work with a Mrs Poppy and about six weeks later with a farming family. I could be doing anything from cleaning to gardening and decorating. Mrs Poppy was a retired child psychiatrist. She used to be a headmistress and home economics teacher. I think she enjoyed hearing about my problems and she told me many stories of the island, her late husband, her parents and her life. We got to be quite good friends. I was loyal to her but never felt comfortable calling her by her first name. I think Maureen, or Mo as she liked to be called, was annoyed that I put Mrs P. first.

A few years later I also got work as relief on the pier, operating the ramp and tying the ferry up, though I used to struggle with the heavy ropes. One time near Christmas the pier master was late, so I had to tie both ends up. I rushed back down to the front and slipped on the icy pier, where I did a roll and got straight back up to carry on, with a cheer from the crew.

Later on the captain came over the radio to wish us a happy Christmas and asked if my knees were OK. It wasn't my knees but my palm that stung. Afterwards I thought of the danger that I could have slipped between the ferry and the pier.

I used to take Bonnie with me, and she was quite happy sniffing around the pier. Once she pinched a fish off a boy who had been fishing. I can still picture her now, coming back to me, wagging her tail with this fish in her mouth. I don't suppose the boy wanted it back after that.

I was lucky I didn't get the sack from that job, as one of our neighbours was always making trouble for people and as she walked onto the ferry she said something about Roger and I struck out at her, catching her on her shoulder. She put in a complaint, but fortunately the other guy who was working that day backed me up, saying that I'd tried to grab her to stop her walking on when a lorry was coming off.

At Easter 2000 my mum decided to fly up with the kids, who would be escorted back by airline staff. She met Owen at a service station on the M4. Owen and Don had gone into the gents together, where he told Don, 'If I had my way the kids would never go up there'. But with the court order he had no choice. I can't remember much about their visits. I was always worried about money and spent time with them working as well, even picking winkles to sell, when I should have concentrated on giving them a good time.

It was always heartbreaking to put them back on the plane, and I stayed at the airport until it was out of sight. Owen didn't like the fact that they were escorted and tried to put obstacles in my way, saying certain dates and flights were not convenient. It was before the age of booking online. The travel agents tried to get the cheapest deals for me, which meant inconvenient hours, but he thought I was lying about flights. I tried various other ways such as driving and bussing to Edinburgh, flying to Cardiff and bringing them back myself, but there just was not an easy answer.

One time when we were going to collect them Roger backed a lorry into the rear door of his 4x4. Another time he put the wrong fuel in the vehicle and another he headed for Stromness instead of St Margaret's Hope ferry, wrong way. It just added to the stress, but he did get it sorted and expected me to be grateful for that.

The weather was against us too. It was always rough when they were due up after Christmas, and one time I had to spend two nights in Kirkwall while the kids were stuck in Aberdeen, being well looked after by airport staff. After that I opted to have them twice a year, with an extra week in the summer holidays.

About nine months after moving to the island, we started getting calls from Jake's uncle, who wanted Roger to come and get him. This happened several times, but nothing came of it. I think Jake's uncle used it as a tool to get him to behave. Several months later he did come, and I really looked forward to having him. If I couldn't have my own then I could devote my time to him. Of course Jake was used to having his own way and didn't like the idea of doing a few chores. He was enrolled in Kirkwall Grammar School (KGS) which meant staying in the halls of residence Monday to Friday. Roger never had any cash to give him and I was expected to give him my £12 cash that I'd earned cleaning for a neighbour.

Roger had this way of going on and on to get his own way, difficult to describe unless you have witnessed it. He was very much like a child who goes on and on without the stamping of the feet. I used to resent giving him my money, so in a way I was glad when that little job came to an end and I was in fact working for nothing.

Problems soon started at KGS and things were getting bad at home. All I used to ask for from Jake was on a Friday evening to sort his dirty washing out and put it in the linen basket, where I had nearly two days to sort it, as he came to us with very few clothes. He used to bring it out around midday on the Sunday, when he had to catch the ferry at 3.30!

One Sunday I sent him with a bin bag full of wet clothes, telling him if he had to spend his money on a dryer, then maybe he'd sort the washing on a Friday. It worked, but he threw it down. He must have hated me from that point on, though I considered myself 'being cruel to be kind'.

Things got so bad with Jake that Roger agreed with me to call in social services, after all they are there to help, aren't they? Roger had hit Jake, so they came out on a launch as an emergency. The social worker arrived with a policewoman and they asked to speak to Jake alone. I didn't have a problem with that, but when we were called back into the room I received such a dirty look. I knew Jake had blamed everything on me. He'd even denied the fact that Roger had hit him.

Jake was placed in temporary foster care, and we had to go to a meeting. Roger had little to say for himself at this meeting, and was not his usual self at all. When I did speak, Jake burst into tears. It was well-timed and we felt done on purpose.

I was in the middle of lambing when Roger came home from another meeting with the report of the first meeting. When I'd read it I was stunned. There was hardly anything against Roger, it was all me. I'd really been portrayed as the wicked stepmother. Jake had said he had to do all his own washing and cook his own meals. Even if it was true, it would not have hurt him. We were both put down for not comforting him when he burst into tears, but I had been too stunned to do that.

I sat on the top of the beach for two hours crying, and Bonnie the black lab sat with me all that time. We refused to go to meetings after that and of course that was seen as uncooperative. Even Jake's foster carers could not handle him, and stopped fostering after their experience with him and social services. Jake ended up in Kirkwall's children's home, Cormoron Resource Centre it was called. That didn't work either, so he was sent to a special school back in England, near his mother's family.

Roger's wife Sue was always in the background, so I pressured him to get a divorce. I had to fill in all the paperwork and find the money for that. After getting divorced Roger then wanted to marry me, saying he had to be married. I agreed, as I thought it would give me security and might make Jake realise that I was here to stay. Famous last words!

CHAPTER SEVEN

SECOND TIME AROUND

The wedding was arranged for April 2003 in a hotel. I didn't want any family there as I suppose I was uncomfortable about the wedding and Mum was constantly pleading poverty, so I thought I'd save her the expense of coming up. But I mentioned to my brother that we were getting married and he invited himself. I didn't want him there as I knew he would upset everyone, and I was right. We just invited folk who had employed or helped us in some way on the island.

It was a nice quiet day. My three kids were there but Jake stayed away. Vince, true to form, got drunk, upset everyone and then when someone said something to him he stormed off. He left early in the morning and I didn't bother to get up to say goodbye. Roger insisted paying for everyone to stay over on my credit card!

Just before the wedding I turned forty. I thought our neighbours had arranged a do for me, but it turned out Roger had agreed to pay for that. I also had a hen do around theirs which I expect he arranged too. I got very drunk and spent the next day in bed.

After being with Roger a while, old debts started to catch up with him, domestic bills, a car finance and the tax man. We could not even pay a current telephone bill and they put us on incoming calls only. The kids and I took turns to phone each other on a Sunday. I had to use the village telephone and tell them ours was broken.

In 2001 I ended up taking a five-year loan out to cover Roger's debts. The Peugeot we had come up in was sold for more than I bought it, but we had to get the scratched windscreen replaced, and that was a hassle as we had to wait for a man who came over to mainland Orkney once a month.

I paid off that loan with the money, so the bank considered me a good bet for another. The man who bought my car kept asking about if it had had its timing belt replaced, and Roger had told him it had and expected me to lie for him. I did but I think he knew I was lying, as I was not brought up to lie. Money was that tight and I was not used to owing everyone money. Roger's favourite saying was 'bullshit baffles brains' and he fobbed everyone off. I could not do that, and I'd be honest but make sure they got something every month. We were just about keeping the wolf from the door.

Then Roger wanted to send me down to London to work as an escort! He had a friend who was doing it, he even got as far as phoning her about it! What did he think I was? He cajoled me into having photos taken, naked and in various forms of undress, and sent some off without my knowledge. I received a reject letter from a modelling agency but a guy who took porn photos would have had me. He did sell one photo to a nature magazine, me feeding the lambs naked except for a pair of wellies. I burned the lot one day, apart from two very tasteful ones that don't show anything.

Roger reluctantly got a job on the salmon farm, but he lasted five weeks and for most of that was 'on the sick'. He did get two, sometimes three days a week working for the North Isles haulier, which suited him much better, with a bit of lorry driving and free trips into Kirkwall. The last few years he was there he got a job as council worker, sit in a small council lorry all day.

Roger's sister came up for a bit to see if she'd like to stay, but it soon became apparent that she liked a drink too. She would not even wake to her son crying in the night, sharing the same bed! After a bit she rented the cottage our neighbours were doing up. She got a fright one night when someone was peering in through the window at her, trying to get lucky no doubt. Someone else reported her for driving our car without any insurance, the only thing Roger was careful with. She got stopped by visiting police even though she was on the insurance and she could not be charged. She wanted to go home after that.

Her son's dad was a Greek Cypriot and the rumour went around that she had adopted him from Romania. Roger started to pick on her, which gave me some respite. She was about 14 years younger than Roger so she was very small when he first married and never remembered living with him as a child. I'm glad she saw what he was really like.

Every time I went away to get my kids, Roger took advantage of the situation to buy something, usually another vehicle. He would phone me on my mobile as the ferry was docking and say 'by the way I have bought...' The debts were getting me down. As soon as I thought we were getting somewhere, it was something else. I'm sure it was a question of 'I want, I will have and I might think about paying for it later'. He kept running up huge shop bills on tick. The manager would present me with bills of £300 plus, I tried to get them to stop letting him put it on account, but it must be difficult to say no and when she was due to retire and wanted to balance the books, she came to me again with another £300-plus bill.

At Easter 2005 when the kids were up, Emily was getting stroppy. It was normally she who followed me around and got involved, but this time she spent most of the time in her room, while Mia helped me. I think Emily thought I was favouring Mia, but if anything I always thought Emily and I connected better, maybe because Mia was a 'Thomas' and Emily was more a 'Brown'. It turns out that Emily had been phoning her dad and saying she wanted to come home. I knew nothing of this until he phoned me himself. They only had five days left but wanted to go, and he could not change the tickets as I'd bought them. He flew up to Kirkwall to get them, which must of cost him a fortune.

Once I realised they were going and did not want to return, I lashed out verbally, and said some awful things. I took them to Kirkwall, put them in a taxi and gave the taxi driver a generous tip to deliver them to their father. I think my son hated me for that. I'd been humiliated enough and I could not face Owen as well.

Alun and Emily refused to even talk to me after that. Mia did for a while and she spent a few days with us near Hereford on a visit to Jake's school, but she refused to go to that, which I was looking forward to. One day Owen phoned me to say she didn't want to talk with me either. At the time I thought pressure had been put on her, but I'm not so sure now.

On this trip south we came back with another 4x4, as Roger had managed to get his own loan for this one. He went mental at someone who nearly drove into it in a car park. One of the things that came to light was me mentioning that they had an older half-sister. I'd always mentioned it now and again and thought they knew, but they claimed that I only told them around the time of mine and Roger's wedding, must have been the only time they remembered. It must have been a shock to them, Alun realising he was not dad's firstborn. It was me that had to pay for his mistake again and he was annoyed that I'd told them, but that was his own fault. If he had mentioned it casually over the years they would have accepted it, like always knowing you were adopted.

Bonnie had bad arthritis and on this trip south Mrs P was looking after her. I'd arranged for some painkillers to be sent over for her but on phoning Mrs P. the next morning, she had asked a farmer to end her suffering. I really expected her to say, 'Oh she is fine now, eating and on her feet'. I really wished I had been there at the end.

Bonnie was buried near the shore on Roger's instructions, although I wanted her in the garden. Sam had long ago been found a new home and they had moved off the island. We lost Bonnie for three days once, and someone found her on a rock in the sea. He had to wade out to lift her off, and she'd lost so much weight that I thought it was Sam for a bit.

With the kids no longer wanting to know me and Bonnie

dead, I knew there was nothing left keeping me in this relationship. I longed to get away but did not know how. Roger was constantly telling me that I had no friends and it certainly felt like it. 'Even your kids don't like you!' he spat at me, and that bit was true. The rows increased so it was every night and I dreaded spending any time with him. I started walking out, but I had nowhere to go and just hoped he'd fallen into a drunken sleep when I returned.

Unknown to me, every time I was walking out he would get on the phone to Owen, my kids' dad, telling him I was cracking up over the abuse I'd had as a kid. Roger always amazed me that we could be having a blazing row and if someone knocked on the door or the phone rang, he was instantly nice, a completely different person, just as if someone had flicked a switch. He had even informed the doctor that I was trying to poison him, though he did most of the cooking anyway.

I found a Dictaphone machine in a kitchen cupboard which he'd obviously used to try recording me saying something, but if he'd got anything I'm sure it would have taped him goading me!

One night I sought refuge with Mrs P. and the next morning he turned up in the council lorry, very apologetic. I went home with him, but he asked me to drop down in the lorry so that no one saw me, in case anyone reported him to the council. While I was ducking down I spotted some of my mail, opened. At home he went for a sleep, as he'd been up most of the night, probably plotting, and I went back to the lorry and retrieved my mail. Next time I was at the island Post Office I asked for my mail to be held, and said I'd collect it in future. When we first came to the island he used to open my mail and seemed to think he had the right. I also caught him reading my diary, where I used to write my innermost thoughts. It was a sense of release for me. 'You're slagging me off all the time' he complained. 'Don't read it if you don't like it'. I stopped writing in them after that.

A few days later he caught me coming out of the shop with my mail, and I knew I was for it when I got home. He stormed into the yard, looking mad. Here we go, I thought. The same verbal abuse, and how bad it looked on him. 'You shouldn't open my mail then!' I retorted. On and on he went, and somehow we ended up in one of the sheds. I couldn't match his constant stream of abuse, so I just stayed quiet, making the odd comment. He advanced on me, pushing me in the upper chest and shoulder. I felt that he was trying to get me to strike him. He'd once hit Jane, Jake's mum, but claimed it was self-defence. I was shit scared and kept backing until I was against the freezer, then all of a sudden he thumped me and I fell to the ground. I was lying there stunned, looking around and trying to figure out how I was going to get out of this. Then he stepped back, burst into tears and said 'look what you have made me do now!'

How was this my fault? After he'd cried his crocodile tears he started again. 'You need to see a doctor' he told me. I did? Surely it was the other way around? 'Even Owen thinks you need help' he said. I argued that he wouldn't, but he said 'I'll prove it to you'. He dragged me into the house and phoned Owen. 'She's at it again Owen' he said. At what, I was wondering?

He handed the phone to me. 'Owen, can you phone the police please, he has hit me!' I said. That stumped Owen for a second but then he kept going on and on about how I needed to see a doctor, seek help because of the abuse I'd received from my dad. I told him I'd hardly thought of that for years and I could not believe what I was hearing. I left it, saying I would go to see the doctor.

That night I slept in the spare room, but I hardly slept at all. I kept thinking, both my husbands say I am cracking up, do they? Having Owen say it had brought doubts in my mind. Maybe it really was me?

If I'd been thinking rationally I would have realised that it was Roger, plotting, covering his own back, and as Owen hardly knew me since we had split how would he know what I was like? Of course it would have been convenient for him, as I'd never have any chance of getting the kids if I was declared unstable.

The next morning I was due at Mrs P's, and as soon as I got there she announced that she had to see the doctor. 'I want to go too' I told her, pulling down my top to show her the two black bruises I had on my shoulder. I told her the events of the night, including what Owen had said, and told her maybe I did need assessing by a psychiatrists. 'Jan' she told me, 'It's him that has the problem, not you'. At this point I did not know what to believe.

We went to the doctor's and Mrs P. let me go first. Fortunately it was a locum and she was very nice. I said 'I'm not ill but I'd like this to be noted on my records' again pulling down my top. I told her the story, including why they thought I was cracking up, which led me to give her a brief outline of the abuse I'd suffered. I asked to be referred to a psychiatrist, but she refused. She told me that she felt I'd dealt with the problem and she ended with saying 'don't be a victim'! Easy to say.

Mrs P. went in next and I expect she told her what she thought. Back at Mrs P's I got on with clearing up the holiday cottage. Then Roger turned up in the council lorry and came over to the cottage. Surely he's not going to start here, I thought. I was relieved to see Mrs P. watching from her conservatory.

'You've called the police, haven't you?' he said.

'No' I replied.

'Yes you have, they have just come out on a launch.'

I told him again that I had not called them. 'But I told the doctor', I said. At this point he stormed off, declaring 'I can't help you now'. Did he really think he was helping me? It was almost funny. Mrs P. was right, he was the one who had the problem.

Mrs P. had suggested that I could move in with her. It was one thing doing a few hours for her, but living with her was a different matter. I also showed the farming family I worked for and the Pier Master my bruises, and his wife Claire jumped down my throat for telling folk. 'Don't you dare go slagging Roger off, why are you doing that?' she said. 'You are supposed to be open about these things these days' I replied. Apparently Claire had been in a violent relationship before and thought she knew everything.

'Are you sure you didn't ask for it?' was her reply. How can anyone ask to be hit? I knew then that they were not my friends and would not help me escape Roger and the only way off the island was on the ferry, I could not even sneak away, and certainly could not be seen taking anything with me.

For months I had been doing some dry stone dyking. I had first continued a wall of about nine meters and I was two thirds of the way into building a 39-meter wall, but I knew I had to go and only the thought that I might never finish this wall made me sad, as I wanted to leave a legacy. In the end I did finish it and hid a little box containing some photos, a few coins of new and old money and a bit of information. I was so scared of Roger catching me hiding this box that I could not say how things were or put my name as Thomas. I'd never really adopted his name but he had the cheek to tell our doctor that I was now an Arnold and informed the bank and car insurance. My passport and driving licence were still in the name of Thomas.

My wall was not that straight and a bit wide in places, but people said it would last a hundred years or more, longer if it was maintained. I got the contract to mow the council grass areas, and it was a job to fit it all in. I tried to get the refuse collection contract but failed, good job really, and twice I went for the post-delivery job. The first time they all thought I'd get the job with previous experience but I was never any good at presenting myself at interviews. The second time an Orcadian got it.

We had had a few fall-outs with the them over them not paying for grass keep, and they had accused us of blocking access to their land, so when he got the post job, Roger was soon on the phone to the Post Office, trying to put doubt in their mind in employing him and trying to lose him his job. My brother had offered to come to get me, but I was afraid he would half-kill Roger and end up inside himself.

So how do you escape a small island when you don't have any friends to help? Now I know that I could have contacted the Women's Refuge or maybe even the police to escort me off the island. It would have been a lot simpler, but when you are frightened, don't have any friends and your husband is so good at appearing to be a great guy and you are seen to be the volatile one, it's not so black and white.

The only thing he said he would not put up with is if I had an affair. I even approached one of the farmers, but he chickened out. He ended up with a girl about forty years younger than him.

Our island was chosen as a test centre for wave energy, as the tides were very strong around the island. This led to some workmen coming over. I was often covering on the pier and one guy, Jim, started to make excuses to be at the pier regularly. It took me a while to realise that he liked me, but I'd guessed when he had tried to get a piece of machinery on the ferry and there was no room, so he said he would try again for the next sailing.

'That one doesn't go on a Sunday' I told him.

'Oh well the next one then, I don't mind as long as you are here' he said.

He was staying at the farm I was working at and I was cleaning the rooms. I left him a message with my number.

Nothing happened until after the new year 2006, when Roger and I had another row. I used that as an excuse to say I was going into town, not realising that everything shuts down at that time of year. I got a room, a single, but changed it for a double and had a night of passion with Jim.

I went back the next day – I was sore and didn't think I could manage another night. Roger seemed happy to see me but he quickly got suspicious and started to follow me. I only got together with Jim one other time when the farmers went away, but we were nearly caught by one of their son's girlfriends.

Later I met him just for a kiss, unaware that Roger had been watching us through the binoculars. I had the 4x4, but he'd borrowed Claire's car and shortly after I headed home, he met me on the single track road. In the car he had a crowbar and went off to find Jim. I'd phoned him to warn him, so his workmates hid him. Roger had taken the keys off me, so I was walking back, intending to go to Mrs P's. Having given up on finding Jim, Roger had turned back and stopped to pick me up. At first I refused to get in. He said he'd take me to Mrs P's but of course he didn't. He hit me as he was driving, though it was nothing compared to last time. He was on about how I was fucking it up for him.

We arrived home in a torrent of abuse and while this was going on, Jim turned up to face him. Roger took his teeth out and Jim took his glasses off, and Roger laid into him before he'd even got out of the vehicle. I was horrified to see my lover just take it. He never once made any attempt to defend himself or fight back, and then after that Roger invited him in to clean up. How strange is that, thump hell out of someone then invite him in!

After a load more of Roger's bullshit, Jim left. Roger was straight on the phone to his boss saying he wanted him off the island. Then he started on me. He wanted me gone, he said. 'Don't worry I'm going' I said and went to pack, but he kept bursting into the bedroom having another go. He opened the bottle of bubbly I was saving and threw the contents of the glass over me. He smashed the bottle and for one moment I thought was going to shove it in my face, but instead he fought me for my mobile and smashed that, then he stormed out, jamming the door so that I could not get out.

I was attempting to squeeze out through the narrow window when he came in again and he told me to go just go. This time I did not hesitate. I grabbed my bag and went. I walked to the shop where there was a phone, but I did not have any money on me and there was not a light in the phone kiosk, so I dialled 999. I apologised for doing so but they got the local police to phone me back. I explained the situation and they were concerned for my safety.

'Do you think he will come after you?' they said. I should have said yes, but I said, 'No he has been drinking and won't drive' – still covering for him!

I'd just reached the hostel that was open, but it was being renovated so there was nowhere to sleep. Then Roger turned up and spent what seemed like a lifetime going on and on. Eventually he stormed off again and I left on foot.

On the island there are no trees except in a few sheltered places, and all the land is open with wire fences. He'd turned right out of the hostel, so he was not heading home. I started to walk to the pier. It was February, a cold but dry night, and every time a vehicle came past I dived face down in the ditch, terrified it would be Roger and he would see me. At one point I jumped back onto the road, misjudged it in the dark and twisted my ankle. If he had come along then, he would have caught me sitting in the road in agony.

I carried on, the pain in my ankle almost forgotten in my need to reach the pier. Finally, around 2.30 in the morning, I was there. Now I just had to stay out of sight until 9.30 when the ferry arrived. It was going to be a long wait.

The haulier's lorry cab was open, and I thought of starting

it, but there was no response. The batteries are often disconnected and I had no tools even to attempt anything. I slept a bit but kept waking, frozen, and went into the ladies to warm my hands on the hand dryer.

Around seven in the morning a vehicle turned up and I realised with relief that it was Matt a mutual farmer friend. I tentatively approached him. 'That's where you have been hiding' he said. He told me that Roger had been to their place a few times even at 4am, crying. He told me to get in. 'Don't worry, I'm not taking you back', he said.

We parked on a beach until it was time for the ferry, and he took a walk and let me use his mobile phone. I tried Jim a few times, and left messages apologising to him. I had warned him of what Roger would do if he found out, but it hadn't stopped him. I also tried to phone Mrs P. to say I wouldn't be in today but she would not answer. No doubt she had received a visitor or two and had many a call.

Matt saw me safely on to the ferry. I expected to see Roger there, but no sign of him. Jim also got the ferry, with two very black eyes. I sat by him but he ignored me and soon found somewhere else to sit. So that's the way of it, I thought, you're on your own now girl.

I walked off the ferry, keeping to myself, Jim caught me up and asked if I was going to stay in a hotel for a night or two. 'No' I stated. 'I'm going to declare myself homeless!'

The first thing I did was buy a new cheap mobile. The women's refuge office was closed, so my next stop was the council offices. I got an appointment for the afternoon. The refuge office was still locked, so I got the courage up to phone, and someone came within half an hour. I had to pour out the details and was taken to the new refuge, where I was put into one of their units. It was brand new and I was the first person in the flat.

One of the first things they got me to do was phone my mum, but I could not remember her number, and all my numbers were in the smashed mobile back on the island. She was ex-directory and it took several attempts before I got hold of an aunt who could give me her number. She told me that Roger had phoned her telling her to sort her daughter out, and she had told him it was up to us to sort ourselves out. It was not the first time he had phoned her.

It turned out that Roger had gone through my address book phoning everyone who mattered to me. In the years to follow, I lost quite a few friends and I'm sure it was down to him, though only one told me he'd been on the phone.

I put in many requests to have my address book, and eventually he sent me an old one that was out of date. Another thing that had been going on in my last year on the island was that I was getting some funny texts. They were of a sexual nature and the sender kept asking me to reply. Thankfully I never did. After a bit the person signed himself as Tom. The only Tom I knew on the island was one of eight siblings. This family kept to themselves, so I had no idea if he'd be like that. I came so concerned about these texts that I reported them to the police.

Emily had phoned me that first Christmas after the split from them, but slammed the phone down on me when I'd got upset. She sent me a few texts after that, one saying 'and Tom is a prick'! Oh my god I thought, these texts are from a friend of hers and the police are about to pay Tom Tait a visit.

We were on our way into town when the police car came out, but I managed to stop him to say it's a friend of my daughters. While I was in town I popped into the police station and the PC tried phoning the number, but it was switched off, as it would be if they were at school. He phoned again, this time leaving a message saying 'This is PC so and so of Kirkwall Police station, regarding the texts you have been sending Mrs Arnold, we know your name and what school you attend, if they don't stop you will be receiving a visit'! I never had another.

I've yet to find out why Emily gave him my number in the first place. She had also sent me a few nasty texts herself, saying she was using my photo on her dart board and if I ever hurt Mia she would kill me. Owen may have been happy to go along with Roger claiming I was cracking up and had problems – if so, like mother like daughter. When I mentioned the texts to him one day, he said what do you expect!

I had started writing my life story in my first Orkney home, with an old PC, and had a lot of it printed out. Obviously I could not be honest about the situation on the island. I hoped to produce a book to sell and I continued the story in fantasy, even making up a lesbian relationship with a woman on the island. Roger just wanted to watch!

After I fled he went around showing various bits to certain islanders, so they all knew about the childhood abuse, and he used it to 'confirm' that I had problems. I kept asking for it back via my solicitor, but he eventually claimed he'd burnt it, probably before he moved the future Mrs Arnold number five in. He met her on the internet, and she was from one of these countries bordering Russia, I think it was Kazakhstan. I only know that she was older than him, had cancer and came with an 18-year-old who she claimed to be her daughter but everyone thought was her granddaughter!

A couple moved just down the road from us, and they stood out a mile, wearing shell suits, she in high heels and him with a cane, acting as lord and master. He talked of having water buffalo, which got the farmers up in arms with the risk of infections. I took an instinct dislike to them. Something was not right, but he wanted Roger as his farm manager. He only had a few more acres than us, and what did Roger know about managing? He had to creep around them, even getting me out of bed one night to play hostess, not one of my strong points. Roger had put them in the second living in room and my first words were 'you, out'! I was speaking to the dog, but this guy jumped. Roger was at their beck and call 24 hours, but I kept away. They had paid for the croft in cash, very suspicious.

Then a few weeks later seven police arrived from Liverpool and chased the guy along the cliff. It turned out he was a conman, and he got three years. The woman's son-in-law was a well-known footballer. She was taken in by him and married him in prison but I believe they later divorced. We sold our story to a Sunday paper. Roger also had a court appearance over causing a breach of the piece by having a go at these two on the ferry. Some years later this guy was again in the paper. This time he had got involved with celebrity and was going to breed pink rabbits. I believe he disappeared with millions of hers. The doctor had lots of cats and her cleaner said they were all over her house. Occasionally one would get run over, in fact I ran one over in the fog - it was right in front of me before I could react, sorry puss.

Someone staying with Mrs P. came back in a panic, saying he had killed one of her cats and asking what he should do with it. 'Where is it?' asked Mrs P. 'In the boot of my car.' 'Well, bury the cat and burn the collar! She will never know'.

I also ran over a dog. They lived on the approach to Mrs P's with the grandparents on either side of the road. I always came through there slowly as they had a little boy and he could have run across the road at any time, but while I was looking out for the boy, I didn't see the dog. He had a broken jaw, and they reported it to the police before I had chance to - it's still a requirement to do so in Scotland. I had a visit from the police over that but no action taken. Did they really think I had run over the dog on purpose?

CHAPTER EIGHT

ON MY OWN AGAIN

The next few days were a whirl of sorting things out. Someone took me shopping, but I was embarrassed to have them buy me clothes. Most of it was from the charity shops, but they drew the line at underwear. I signed on, but soon got a job driving for a local taxi firm. Roger kept phoning the refuge, sending me letters and faxes. He kept asking for me to phone him, and concerned he was annoying the refuge staff, I did phone him, not from my mobile but a payphone. He went on and on, not slagging me off this time but begging me to come home. I kept saying I had to go and the only way I could get off the phone was to say I'd think about coming home, but I had no intention of doing so.

Matt met me in town one day and told me Roger had gone around saying I was begging to come home and he was thinking of letting me come back! I laughed. It just reminded me that I'd done the right thing. And he was going to report me to the tax man for undeclared earnings, what a saint!

Once I was walking to the shops and came across him.

Possibly he was waiting for me. He had a right go, but as soon as someone passed, again it was a nice smile and pleasantries.

I filed for divorce, but under Scottish law the finances have to be sorted out first. I wanted to go to court to get an order for the house to be sold. We had bought it for fifty grand but prices had shot up since we had moved. He made things as difficult as possible and in the end I took the settlement offered just to get rid of him, but I did insist on him signing a statement to say he had abused me verbally and hit me. He tried to be seen as generous in the settlement, saying he'd given me a bit more than half the value and a payment of £750 for doing the dry stone dyking, when I knew he had received thousands for it in a grant!

Shortly after the divorce he married his Russian woman. He sold the house for £170,000, paid me a fraction of that and they moved to Bulgaria, where at the time you could buy a place for about £12,000. He must have felt very pleased with himself. My solicitor said afterwards that I had a good case to go to court, but I wish she had given me that confidence before.

I invested most of my money in the market, and it was just my luck that everything crashed within a year. I can still see the financial advisor looking me in the eye and saying 'I will treble your money in seven years'! Roger also kept things that he had bought for me, like the computer. 'I paid for it, it's mine' he said, but he also kept the things I had paid for like the fax machine, metal detector and dishwasher. When I mentioned the loan I'd taken out to get everyone off his back it was 'that's your problem'. Fortunately it only had six months left.

After getting him out of my life I was saving again and even bought myself a car for cash out of my wages. Things were on the up. We had mutual friends who had moved off the island the year before us. I thought she was a good friend, but her husband did not want me to come round. He was not impressed with my infidelity but it was all right for Roger to strike me. I did see her in the town but I was annoyed that I did not get support from them. It was fine for Roger to come around, but they were not keen on him bringing the new Mrs Arnold, the language being the main problem. I used to think at least if he tried his tactics of putting her down, she wouldn't understand him as she didn't speak much English and he could rant on and on to no effect.

Roger would phone them regularly and at one time tried to get them to put him and his wife up. Lea didn't want to but he went on and on. I think Lea got a taste of what he was like. To put him off, Lea had to admit that she had cancer of the womb and was not fit for visitors. She didn't want anyone to know and asked him not to tell anyone but of course he did, everyone knew except me.

Thankfully Lea is OK after having a hysterectomy, and she has never wanted children. She tells me the last she heard from Roger was when he phoned her at home asking about taking some money out for his wife's funeral, and she was not dead at the time!

Lea worked at his bank, and she was annoyed that he'd phoned her at home. Last time she asked me 'Have you heard from Roger Arnold', it took me a while to think who he was! That was a good sign, I was putting the bad experience behind me.

Roger and I did have a few joint accounts, and I had quite a job to get my name off them – I'll never have a joint account again. After Roger used my childhood abuse against me, I no longer tell my partners about it.

I did not enjoy being a taxi driver and having to pick up drunks who thought it was all right to have their hands on my leg. We did not even get the minimum wage but were given a third of our takings.

I approached the local bus company, as I'd been told they were putting people through their tests. I wandered up one day and spoke to their controller, and he gave me a form to apply for my provisional, but first you had to have a medical. I did not think I would pass on my eyesight, but I think he felt sorry for me and passed me. After this I was determined to get my eyes lasered.

I started having lessons with a volunteer driver, and after a while he turned us over to a qualified driving instructor. I found him a bit sarcastic at times. Also learning at the same time was another woman and a man. The man had to be told no more driving, he was dangerous. The instructor said that I and the other woman learning with me were better than some of the men who had been there for years.

My test was set for July that year, 2006, but I failed miserably, and the examiner actually stormed off. I failed to notice a car coming along a narrow road I was about to turn into, and the other driver could not reverse and nearly went into the ditch. I said to the examiner 'I guess that's a fail'.

'You should have waited at the junction, but carry on anyway' he said.

When we were heading back to the test centre, I braked sharply, not sure if someone was going to use the crossing. The examiner was not looking. He was doing his paperwork and nearly fell off his seat.

I also failed the reverse test. The instructor said he'd never seen him storm off before!

I reapplied for the following month, the 22nd, more nervous than the first time, but fortunately for me the examiner had fallen off his motorbike and broken his collar bone so he was off sick and I took the test with his stand in. This man put me at ease. We went to the mart to do the reverse manoeuvre, which meant parking on the right and having to do a zigzag manoeuvre over to the left and parking in a space without touching the bar. When this guy set it up, I told him that he had not left enough room. He measured it again and thought he had and asked me to try it, but then he stopped me, saying, 'You're not going to do it'. He moved the cones and this time gave me too much room, but I didn't tell him so. This time I passed with only a few minor gear change marks against me.

I started driving the next day, but I did not join them full time until October after getting an employment contract. I tried to still do one night a week on the taxis but found it too much with twelve-hour-plus days.

Just before I started on the buses full time, I went to Aberdeen to have my eyes lasered. It was not painful to have done, but it was frightening and my eyes felt really gritty afterwards. For the first week, I could see perfectly in the morning but my eyes would deteriorate through the day. I had to get glasses again and have had my prescription changed several times since. I can see a lot better than I used to - in fact I could only see clearly about four inches in front of my face but now I can see my feet when I shower!

In a way I'm glad that I still have to wear glasses as I have permanent 'black eyes'. One optician did suggest I was allergic to something, but now I think it's hereditary, it seems to be worse in me. My nan, Dorothy Pearson, had it, and my mum has too.

The last time I saw Roger, he was standing outside the post office in Kirkwall. I was driving one of the new long low-floor buses and there were road works and a diversion in place, so I had to make a tight turn. Thankfully I did it perfectly and it made me smile knowing that could be his last memory of me. He had tried to stop the manager from employing me - he phoned her and said 'Don't employ her, she will cause nothing but trouble'. Thankfully she was prepared to give me a chance.

I've been there well over seven years, not without some problems, but they are saved for another book after I've retired.

In 2010 Jake Arnold sent me a Facebook request. I've nothing against the lad but that would have given Roger access to what I'm up to, so I never accepted and even blocked him for a while. The frightening thing about all this is not Roger trying to claim that I was cracking up but knowing that if I'd have stayed with him then I would have cracked up - he would have driven me to it!

I felt lonely on my own. Jim contacted me in the refuge, but only to warn me that his wife might be paying me a visit. Roger had not let up until he'd got hold of his wife to tell her. They lived at the back of my friend Lea's house and out driving I saw them sometimes. I noted that she had made an effort with her appearance. He did visit me once when I had a flat, drunk and hoping for a night of passion, but I was involved with someone else by then. I still wave to him when we pass, and I'll always be grateful to him for getting me away from Roger.

I had a few dates, but no one took to me being so quiet. Then I started seeing Gareth, who did the odd night on the taxi radios. He was three years younger than me and I was warned against him as he was known for violence, but I was prepared or perhaps desperate enough to give him a chance. As always things are fine at first. His family were into bingo, something I associated with retired folk. I tried it but could not see what they saw in it, and they went three times a week!

While I was seeing him the council gave me an emergency flat, in Kirkwall's only 'high rise' flats, which were three floors. The flat had only one bedroom but was quite spacious, and I would have liked to stay there.

Gareth was spending so much time with me that one day he announced that he had moved in. I didn't want him to, but again I found it difficult to say no. By this time he was back to his old ways of staying out most of the night, coming home drunk in the early hours and wanting to talk, which had me going to work knackered when I was due up at 5.30 am.

At Christmas Gareth bought very cheap, tacky wedding and engagement rings, as he intended to ask me to marry him! He never really asked but blurted out his intentions while drunk sitting at the bar. Helen, who I'd become friends with, was trying to get me to say yes, but this was a definite NO.

We were now living in a smaller flat right by the cathedral. The bedroom was so narrow that I had to buy a four-foot bed. As soon as we moved in Gareth wanted me to apply for a bigger flat, as it was only supposed to be me living there. I tried to hint to Gareth that it was not working and he should leave, but he was not getting the message.

Then someone else started to chat me up. He was another charmer but I don't think he was nasty with it. He told me he liked me but obviously didn't want to see me while I was with Gareth. I sat down and wrote Gareth a long letter trying to get the message over. Apparently he took this letter to show his mum, and after reading it she said he'd better come home.

But he did not give up. I was due to go to my niece's 18th back home, and I'd already paid for us both to fly down. I was nervous of going on my own so I let Gareth come as a friend. I told my family the situation, but he was still trying to be a couple and tried it on a few times, then spent the night slagging me off to my brother. It was a long week and I could not wait to get home and away from him.

A few weeks later I was due to go to a 40th birthday party for one of the female drivers. I received a text from Gareth asking me if I wanted to go to some do at the Masonic Hall, and texted back 'no thanks I have a date'. He took that to be another man and saw red. Next thing I know he was hammering on my door, wanting me to let him in, but with his record of violence I refused. He started going on about a mirror of his that I still had, he'd won it in one of the bingo raffles. When he went around to the side window I grabbed the chance to put the mirror outside the door, hoping he would go away. He was now telling me that if I didn't let him in he would break in. By this time I was so scared that I rang the police, and I had to give directions to the sergeant. He was just walking up when he heard the window smash and caught Gareth half way through it. The policeman arrested him and shouted to me that he would be back to take a statement. Gareth had no choice but to plead guilty. He had threatened to drive into my bus if I did not continue to see him and he kept following the bus and another woman driver who perhaps looked a bit like me.

He got put on a tag with a curfew imposed and a box was inserted in my flat that would warn them if he came close. A few months later he had punched his sister and moved one of the taxis while drunk, so he lost his licence again and got sent down. He wrote to me from the prison, asking me to get back together and to write back with my phone number. I hadn't changed my number so I did wonder if the police had deleted it from his phone. I never wrote back.

Helen was also having a problem, with a man called Raymond. She was too nice to tell him where to go. He turned his attentions on me, and one day I came home to flowers and a gift on my doorstep. I posted the gift through his door with a note making it clear that I would go to the police if he didn't stop bothering me. I didn't put it very nicely and didn't put it in an envelope, knowing his father would probably see it before him, but it didn't bother me again. I do seem to attract them!

So Stan started to come around. He also was living with someone and over the next year I heard all the excuses under the sun as to why he couldn't get her out. After a bit it became clear that he was bullshitting me, but it really hit me one day when he came over while I had Helen around. He popped to the bathroom and came out naked. He only expected us to have a threesome!

I think Helen would have gone for it but I certainly did not fancy her. I was really taken aback by this. Helen left us to it and he tried to convince me that he was only joking!

Soon after this I started seeing James, a single part-time dad who had been beaten by his estranged wife - she had knocked him through the window of a mobile home. He had a two-bedroomed council house. He was a lovely guy, but it only lasted about five weeks as even though his wife was sleeping with every man that would have her, she did not want him to see me. She threatened me and would get their five-year-old girl to thump me as hard as she could. I had to get out of there, otherwise I would have snapped and hit the girl.

It came to a head when I'd spent an evening with Helen and got the late bus back. He'd left the door unlocked for me but in the morning he asked me to sneak out when he was giving the kids their breakfast and ring the doorbell as though I had just arrived. His wife had said she didn't want me staying over with the kids there. I had a hangover, and with another bashing from the five-year-old that was the last straw, so the next day I told him it was over. We have remained friends. I believe he now has custody of the kids, four of them now. The fourth has his name but can't be his as he had a vasectomy and he now has another girlfriend.

So Stan and I resumed our relationship. I waited in that Christmas as he'd promised to come over. Helen had invited me over and I turned up really late – I should have known better than to waste the day. He went quiet for a few days, not answering my texts, and then texted that he'd got drunk and had got engaged! I texted back, 'well you better get disengaged!'

He did say he would never marry her, but is that supposed to make it all right? What with the engagement and the fact that he'd let it slip out that things were getting boring and with rumours that he was visiting a few other women, it was inevitable that we were on our way out, though I really liked him and still held a hope that things would change.

I wonder if all men who have the gift of the gab have small dicks. Both Roger and Stan did, but perhaps what they lack in the trouser department they make up with their mouths!

There was a guy at work, Len, who I thought liked me, though I didn't get on with him at first. I'd met his estranged wife and she was spreading lies that he had hit her. I went out with her and Helen a few times, and it soon became clear that she was not quite the ticket. I can remember her saying 'Oh Helen, you have got to look after me'. I told her she was old enough to look after herself. The dentist had to break her jaw once for treatment, and she told everyone that Len had done it. I noticed that when I did have something to say in the tea room he stopped in mid-sentence to listen to me, and he always seemed to be willing to help with any problems. So when I asked him over to sort something out with a bus, I took the plunge and asked him if he'd like to go for a drink.

It started from there. Soon I was staying over on a Saturday night, at first in the spare room. After six months Len asked me to move in with him. I was flattered to be asked but I thought hard about it. Did I really want to go down that road again? Maybe it was the drunks walking past the flat and the cathedral bells keeping me awake, combined with the fact that his bungalow was in the country in a very quiet area, that made me go for it. He already had my cat staying there. She had been hit by a car and broke her leg in two places, which cost me over £300, and then they wanted to amputate it for another £170. I wouldn't let them, and she only has a slight limp now.

CHAPTER NINE

ANOTHER TRY

I moved in with Len in October 2008. It's his house and I pay him rent and some bills. I paid for a landline to be put in and broadband, and it seems to work. I don't want to get married again but I'd like to be asked, just for him to show me that he likes me enough. Sometimes I still feel like a lodger, that I'm just here to help him financially. Now and again he talks of selling up and getting something smaller, but I'm not so sure it would work living in a two up, two down in Kirkwall.

In contrast to Roger, Len has always said I am too independent and can look after myself. It's not been without its problems. He has a daughter, Stephanie, and I would not even stay over without her approval. She first lived with her mum but she was not looking after her basic needs of food and bedding, so Steph used to pinch towels, bedding and toilet rolls from us. Len once refused to let her stay with her mum as she had no bedding for her. I decided not to get involved with her after the experience with Jake, but it's been very frustrating and still is to do a twelve-hour day and find that she can't be bothered even to sort the dishwasher out – it's not as though I am asking her to do it by hand. She does not lift a finger in the house, though it's not really her fault when she has not been brought up to do anything.

I used to try to clean her bedroom up, and I'd find bloodied knickers in boxes and every time I'd do it she would sulk for ages. Being tidy did not feel comfortable to her. I used to think that her mother or aunts were doing her washing, as only the odd thing was put in the wash, but if she did put a pair of jeans in the wash they were that stiff that I could stand them up on their own, like cardboard, being that dirty.

I occasionally mentioned it to Len and he would hunt for dirty clothes or have a spree where everything was washed. Steph did attend the dentist regularly, which was only over the road from the school – maybe it was a way to skip classes. Her dentist reported her to the social for her personal hygiene – it can't be very nice getting really close to someone when they stink.

Len had a visit from the social worker and I kept well away this time. I got him to text me when it was OK to come home. He did mention me and she said they were aware of me!

Once Steph came through to say £5 had gone missing from her piggy bank, and I asked if she was accusing me of taking it. 'It's only me, dad and you here' she said. 'Don't put me on the same footing as your mother!' I bit back, and she stormed off.

Carol had not paid the mortgage or the domestic bills, and she left with Stephanie knowing the bailiffs were coming around to repossess the house. Len's mum helped him out and he is still paying her off. A few days later I was handed back a pink child's purse which I had found on my bus a few months before, which contained a few pounds. I planted it in Stephanie's room to see if she would say 'I don't know where this purse has come from'. She found it but never said a word. Like her mother, she has a problem with holding onto money.

Stephanie is 18 now and still has to be nagged to take a shower. At times she smells as bad as these dirty old men we get on the bus, and her boyfriend is worse. For Christmas I bought him some shower gel, deodorant and a book titled 'Personal hygiene, what's that got to do with me?' Not feeling able to broach the subject, I also put in a note saying that if he was frightened to tell his dad he's dirty, I will. His dad sent me a threatening message via Facebook. Anyone else would have thanked me and done something about it!

We hoped she would change when she got a boyfriend. He is only four months older than her, they get on well, they are engaged (third time for Stephanie) and it may work as she just wants a man to do her bidding and she has that in Adrian. I gave up trying to give her advice as I was just getting told to 'fuck off, you are just dad's girlfriend'. At least she didn't say 'lodger'. Since she turned sixteen, when in Scotland they are 'adults', she only spends the odd night or three here, usually when she wants something. She flits between her mother's and his father's. I think it has just got through to her that you have to work for money. She is fortunate to have aunts who have a music school, shop and café. Her aunts are semi-famous. Maybe the kid lacks love and is desperate for it, had a bit of a rough time and I have not helped, not having that rapport with kids.

She has just moved into a flat and the family are concerned that Adrian will not pay his way. I think it will be the making of them, after the honeymoon period wears off and they realise that it's a hard slog paying bills.

In the autumn of 2010, I started researching my family tree. A cousin had extensively looked into the Brown side, so I concentrated on the Pearson side. I was disappointed not to find any links to anyone famous, but I'm sure if I followed every branch line, there would be some.

I did find a few 'skeletons'. You expect to find a few references to 'father unknown' but there is one 'mother unknown', along with the story of a woman coming from Scotland dumping her child on a family and saying the child was his. My grandmother, Dorothy Pearson, née Bunt, always said she was one of ten with twin brothers, but I cannot find her siblings with the same birth date. She would never talk about her family. Her mother died when she was a baby and she was raised by her eldest brother. Apparently her mother spent a short spell on the stage, but in those days, stage girls were seen as prostitutes and we were told she married her Manager. In the 1911 census, her husband was only a porter at the Palace Theatre.

The most interesting person would have been her brother, Frederick Bunt, who was a photographer with the *Evening Standard* and photographed the Beatles. Unfortunately he died in the 70s and I cannot find any trace of him marrying or having children. Now I would have loved to talk to him about and his life and travels. Perhaps when I retire I will look into the family more extensively.

Back in the women's refuge, I had a chat with the family mediation service and they wrote to my son via Owen, but they did not even reply to the letter. Over the years I tried all sorts, letters, phone calls, and never forgot birthdays.

When the girls turned sixteen I received a letter from the school saying that now they were sixteen, they had asked the school not to send me their reports or give out any information about them. The school had even consulted a solicitor on the matter. It felt as if the knife had been inserted a little deeper and given a twist. But what could I do? I did reply to the school saying I'd accepted the decision, as someone had to be adult here. I just continued with the birthday and Christmas cards, sending cheques. Sometimes they were cashed, sometimes not.

I did find out from a school report that Emily had been seriously ill. Later I found out that she had had pneumonia plus complications. I often wondered if anyone would have informed me if she had she died – I doubt it.

I could never understand him keeping me out of it. Even when they were living with me, he once took them to Ireland and did not return them on the given day. Even his parents did not know why they were late and when I asked him about it he just said 'it's none of your business'. My children don't forget. I wish I'd reported it to the police.

He never consulted me on anything. If they had lived with me I would always have asked his opinion, even when the girls wanted their ears pierced. They have turned out lovely kids apart from following him in not wanting to know me. I just wonder if they would have turned out even better if he had included me in their lives, and I also wonder how they will treat their partners if they split with children.

I made the decision to go down for the girls' 18th. There was no way that I could say I was coming down, as they would not agree to see me. Len decided to come too and I think his family wanted us to take Stephanie, but this was time for my kids – I'd rather have gone on my own than take her. She went to stay with her grandmother, who is a teacher, and fell out with granny, who was trying to get her to pull her weight. We made a bit of a holiday of it, travelling down the west coast, and spent a few days on the Isle of Skye and in Yorkshire. Then we went to my mum's and took her with us to Wales.

We had borrowed one of Len's sister's cars, a Rover, the model that looks like a Jag. It broke down when we got to Saundersfoot. I had just phoned Willie Williams to say we were on our way. Len decided not to get his hands dirty, but we had AA cover. We were taking it to a garage at a farm in St David's and got B & B for the night while the car was being repaired. It had only thrown a belt.

The lady who was running the B & B said her granddaughter was also 18 tomorrow – we were probably all in Withybush Hospital together. The car would not be fixed for ages, so Mum and I decided to go the rest of the way on the bus. There were plenty of buses from St David's to Haverfordwest, but only a few from Haverfordwest to Carmarthen. Then it would mean a two-mile walk from the main road to where my three lived.

Willie came to the rescue and offered to drive us there. He didn't have to, and I can't thank him enough to coming to my rescue once again. We planned to arrive around eleven in the morning, but as we pulled up over the road from the house, Emily crossed the road in front of us and waved! She later told us she thought we were her neighbour. Having not seen them for over six years it took me a second to realise it was her.

We got out of the car, and Willie said he would hang around

for ten minutes in case we needed a lift back. I knocked and Emily opened the door. 'Happy Birthday Ems' I said. 'Oh my god we did wonder if you would come today!' she said. We were allowed in and there were hugs. Mia was having a shower and Alun was out taking a walk. Emily welcomed us, so did Mia, and when Alun returned from his walk, he went to go upstairs and I called out. 'Hello son' I said, more hugs. I could not believe how tall he was. He towered over me and must tower over his father.

We had a really pleasant afternoon. Unfortunately the village pub was closed so I couldn't buy the girls their first legal drink. Emily made us a sandwich. Len got a bit lost but found us in the end. Our O2 phones did not work very well there. The girls did offer me their phones, but I didn't want them pressured into giving me their numbers, especially after those texts I had had from Emily.

Their father came home about 2.30. They had warned him I was there but as soon as he arrived the atmosphere dropped. Everyone noticed, and we didn't stay long after that. Len did take some group photos of us all which I treasured, even sending copies to Willie and posting them on my Facebook page.

Here my story should end on a happy note with a lovely man and a reunited mother and children, but it was not to be. Things were fine for a year, and I started paying money into the girls' accounts to help with their further education. Mia went to university to study sport and exercise science and said she wanted to be a sport physio. Emily was doing photography and drama, while Alun was working in hotels, doing bar work and waiting, but kept saying he wanted to go to flying school.

We started speaking on the phone again, though it was always me who had to phone, and there were emails. Several times I had requested to be their Facebook friends to no avail. I don't think Alun is on it, or maybe I am blocked.

Our next trip south was planned for September 2012, fifteen months after the twins' 18th. They kept saying to let them know when I was coming down, and I think Owen made a big thing about me just turning up. I duly kept saying we were coming in September and nearer the time I said we would be at their Nan's around the 16th and would phone from there. The week before I had an email from Emily saying she was moving in with her boyfriend then and it wouldn't be convenient. When I asked for her new address she said 'why, are you just going to turn up?' and when I said 'I won't do that, but surely I can turn up with a potted plant', she never replied.

Two days before we were due to travel I had an email from Mia saying she would be back at university then, although I thought she wasn't due back until the following week. She said she didn't feel she was at a stage when she wanted to see me again. This email had come through to my phone at work. I was so upset that another driver had to do a run for me. I felt like I had died, in fact I wanted to die. I emailed Alun saying 'if you want to see me give me your mobile number'. Of course I don't know if he received that email or not, but I never had a reply.

We had our holiday anyway and I made the best of it. For Stephanie we stayed at Alton Towers, but she would not go on anything and spent the whole time sulking, possibly because Adrian was not with us, but we couldn't be expected to pay for him as well. It was only a few days before we went that we knew she was coming. She spent the whole time texting and on the phone to various people, obviously slagging us off, as she kept having to go out the room or would say 'I can't talk now'. I vowed not to take her again.

The only day she enjoyed was a trip to Cotswold Wildlife Park. Living in Orkney she had never seen these animals in the flesh before, and she was like a little kid saying 'Daddy, Daddy, come and look!'

Because Stephanie was with us, even Mum was not prepared to put us up. When we got home she had been nagging to go to her mum's first, but Len insisted on dropping our luggage at home first. I went through all sorts of emotions over my three. Upset, anger, how dare they? I think if Mia had been standing in front of me I would have slapped her. She was the one who I thought would do anything for anyone. How wrong can you be?

I felt this was the last straw, and I had had enough. I will still keep giving her money until she graduates in June 2014, when they turn 21, but that is it then. Their father can truly say I am not bothering. I would never have cut him out of their life had they been with me, but they seem to have inherited a selfish Thomas streak. I try to think what I did wrong this time. Maybe it was having a gripe about Stephanie – I'm sure my girls would have liked her better than me. Maybe it was because I stopped giving Emily money when she finished college, or maybe it was the invitation to Alun to come up for the summer to work in hotels, a change of scene and yes I'd love it if he met someone and wanted to stay.

I used to dream of the kids coming up and surprising me, turning up at work, coming out with me for the day. Maybe Alun flying in and taking me out to lunch on Shetland. I've stopped dreaming now, I doubt it will ever happen and if they do find their conscience later in life it may be too late. I am thirty years older than the girls.

In 2012 my friend Helen went quiet on me and eventually sent me an email saying she felt we could no longer be friends. Deja vu! I'd no idea what I'd done but it turns out that I was not the only person she rejected. She has since friended me again but I'm very reserved about it and don't often see her. Maybe it was because her daughter-in-law blamed her for losing her baby at seven months pregnant. I never received an apology for the way she treated me and I have wondered if she has friended me again to give her driving lessons - I didn't take the hint. Helen also lived on the small island I had moved to with Roger, but her husband kept her to himself, not socialising with any one. They had eight children and she ended up in the women's refuge after me.

Helen got involved with an electrician who came to do some work in her council house. I found him very sleazy and didn't take a liking to him. He also had a live-in girlfriend while carrying on with Helen, and this girl asked me to take some photos of her. After a while it became clear that she wanted semi-naked photos. What the hell, I thought, you carry on. We were in the middle of this when Simon turned up, and I soon realised that this had been planned. He wanted to take photos of the pair of us. I refused and told them, 'I don't care what you get up to, but don't involve me'. He wouldn't let up, so I walked out. His van was blocking my car in, and it crossed my mind to ram it. I shouted from the doorway for him to move it, and he came out, saying "I hope you're not going because of me?"

"Damn right I am!" I replied. I was so angry that I was shaking. How dare they?

Simon's live-in girlfriend eventually left, buying her own house. He openly started a relationship with Helen then, but she found him obsessive. He made her get rid of the dogs, and her kids didn't like him so they split. Only a few months later he married a foreign women he'd met on line, but he still badgers Helen for sex. I'm not sure if she gives in to him.

Vince's first wife got in touch with me via Facebook. I think she still has a lot of issues about being with my brother. She kept going on about the time we were all living with my parents, and something happened. It appears I was drunk and I've no idea what she was referring to but she kept saying 'you know'. At one point I thought she was suggesting that she had slept with Owen, but when I asked her if that was so she got very aggressive, so I had to tell her where to go and unfriended her. She has since tried again to get in contact, but I don't want to go there.

I've tried to come up with ways to 'better myself'. I don't quite have the money to buy my own place, even a one-bedroomed flat. I looked into us buying the store from Len's parents. They would have been happy to sell it to us, but the council was only likely to give permission for one house, and I could only see it working if we could put three or four terrace houses there. I also approached the people who own the derelict house over the road, thinking I could get it for around £35,000, do as much as I could now and then the rest gradually, but she told me she had refused an offer of £95,000 last year, way out of my league.

Why am I writing this? Many reasons – the thought that I may go senile, lose my memory in later life. For my kids, who don't want to know me, and my grandchildren, who may never be allowed to get to know me. For all those women out there who have been abused and put down all their lives from controlling men. To prove that there is life after abuse – we can get through it and survive.

I have just read a book about a slave girl, written over 150 years ago. I'd like to think someone will be reading this in 150 years, and if I do not get it printed I give future generations permission to do so.

Emily once said to me 'It's not all about you'. Of course it isn't. I wish my kids could add to this to put their side, but I have not been allowed to know how they feel.

I had a scare a few months back when a routine scan found some foreign bodies. It turned out to be nothing, but it got me wondering, would I tell my kids? If I did would they feel obliged to see me if I'd been given so long to live? Or would they not even bother then? After all it would make no difference to their lives whether I was alive or not. Owen, like Prince Charles, would benefit most, knowing their mother would never interfere again.

I'd heard of Asperger's syndrome back in the summer when someone approached me on the bus and told me Stephanie was honking and they thought she had Asperger's. I googled it and the list of symptoms did not relate to Stephanie at all, but I did think they seemed to relate to me. After Susan Boyle announced that she had Asperger's, I did an on-line test. I expected it to say I had a touch of it, but I actually rated very high. It makes sense.

I always thought being quiet and not being able to hold a conversation was down to the abuse I suffered, but there are plenty of women out there who suffered far worse than me and they are not all withdrawn. Some are in fact stronger. I now know that if it comes to it, I can survive just fine on my own.

ND - #0502 - 270225 - C0 - 203/127/14 - PB - 9781861512680 - Matt Lamination